DO YOU KNOW

ENGLISH WORD ORIGINS?

From
academy to zodiac

by
DAVID HILLIAM

POCKET REFERENCE BOOKS

A POCKET REFERENCE BOOK

Published by:
Pocket Reference Books Publishing Ltd.
Premier House
Hinton Road
Bournemouth
Dorset BH1 2EF

First published 1996

Typesetting:	Gary Tomlinson PrintRelate (Bournemouth, Dorset) (01202) 897659
Cover Design:	Van Renselar Bonney Design Associates West Wickham, Kent BR4 9QH
Printing and Binding:	RPM Reprographics Units 2-3 Spur Road Quarry Lane, Chichester West Sussex PO19 2PR Tel. 01243 787077 Fax. 01243 780012 Modem 01243 536482 E-Mail: rpm@argonet.co.uk

© illustrations Chambers Harrap Publishers Ltd., Edinburgh

ISBN: 1 899437 44 4

Contents   *Page(s)*

INTRODUCTION

The English language has an unquenchable thirst for new words.

It has assimilated words from every conceivable source. Although the basic vocabulary is derived from Anglo-Saxon, Latin, or Norman French, there's hardly a country in the world which hasn't contributed at least a few words to our ever-expanding language.

We tend to take our language for granted, perhaps without pondering much where it came from. On the whole, people look at dictionaries only for help with spelling or meanings. But there's a world of excitement awaiting you if you look up quite ordinary words simply to find out how we came by them.

We all know what a 'muscle' is. But it comes as an astonishing revelation to find out that muscles get their name because they look like little mice rippling under our skin, with tendons as tails! And the Latin word for a little mouse is *musculus*.

Look up 'daisy' and find that our Saxon ancestors called it the 'day's eye' because it opens and closes so readily according to conditions of sunlight.

Look up 'anorak' and find that it is one of the few words we have taken from the Eskimos of Greenland.

Or look up the flower 'nasturtium' and be intrigued to learn that its literal meaning is 'nose-twister'.

There are over half a million words in our language, and many of them have quite remarkable histories.

I hope you'll enjoy this collection of some of my favourites.

David Hilliam

TEASERS
What do *you* know about English word origins?

The word 'arctic' comes from the name of an animal. Do you know which one?

What pagan god do we unconsciously remember in the middle of the week?

What is the connection between dachshunds and badgers?

Who is remembered in the name of the month of July?

Do you enjoy a glass of 'plonk'? Where do we get this curious word from?

What town in France is 'denim' named after?

And 'jeans' are named after a town in Italy: which one?

Why are monks called monks?

What is the connection between a galaxy and a lettuce?

There is no such thing as a coco tree. So why is a coconut so called?

What Turkish article of clothing are tulips named after?

Why is an unlucky batsman out 'for a duck'?

Why does an unlucky tennis-player score the unlikely total of 'love'?

How does the season of 'Lent' get its name?

Why is a scout called a scout? What special sense does he need?

What firework gets its name from a North African saint?

What colour gives a 'blanket' its name?

What Pacific island is remembered in the name of an article of swimwear?

Nine-carat gold? Well, what exactly *is* a carat?

Where does 'parmesan' cheese come from?

PAKISTAN is an acronym. What do the individual letters stand for?

What is the 'pole' in a 'tadpole'? Come to think of it, what is the 'tad'?

Where do 'spaniels' come from?

What farm animal is referred to in the word 'vaccination'.

Which President of the USA gives his name to the 'Teddy Bear'?

You'll find the answers in the pages that follow

More and more 'acronyms' are being added to our language nowadays. The word 'quango' is made up from the initial letters of Quasi-Autonomous Non-Governmental Organisation! What a mouthful!

But acronyms aren't new. In 1867 a confederation was established, amalgamating the three provinces of Canada, Nova Scotia and New Brunswick, and the problem arose, what to call this 'new' country. Eventually it was decided simply to call it 'Canada'. But among suggestions at the time was the odd name 'Efisga', from the initials of the countries who had colonised it: England, France, Ireland, Scotland, Germany and a final letter to remember the Aboriginal lands. Canada would then have been called 'EFISGA'!

academy

No patch of ground can have made as important a contribution to the vocabulary of scholarship and instruction as the garden outside Athens where Plato taught. The *Akademeia* was a grove, containing a gymnasium, that got its name from the Greek hero Akademos. It was here, in about 387 BC, that Plato set up his school of philosophy. The school too became known as *Akademeia*, a word that, in various forms, passed into international use as a name for schools and other institutions providing training or promoting culture.

So it is to this original 'grove of Academe' that we owe our 'academies' our 'academic' qualifications, our Royal 'Academicians', and so on.

acorn

The 'corn' or fruit of the oak: 'oak-corn'.

According to ancient Scandinavian superstition, Thor, the god of thunder, had a special love of oak trees, and so people would put acorns near a window, so as to protect their homes from lightning.

acre

King Edward I, who reigned 1272-1307, is responsible for standardizing our measure of an 'acre', fixing it in 1305.

It had always been the amount of land which a yoke of oxen could plough in one day, but obviously this was rather a rough sort of a calculation. Edward fixed it at a strip 40 rods long by 4 rods wide. This works out at 4840 square yards.

In these days of metrication, not many people remember the old style of measures. The 'rod' ($5^1/_2$ yards, or $16^1/_2$ feet) was sometimes called a 'pole' or 'perch', and it was in fact the long stick which the ploughman used to drive his oxen. Striding along behind the plough, he needed a long stick or rod to reach over to prod his beasts.

The word 'acre' is simply a version of the Latin word *ager*, a field, the same word which gives us 'agriculture'.

Ever since 1305 fields and gardens have been measured in 'acres' – a word going back virtually unchanged since before the time of Christ.

aftermath

The word 'aftermath' slips easily enough into everyday speech, but few users of it would know exactly what the 'math' is which apparently comes afterwards!

Literally, it is the grass which is mowed. Lawn-cuttings are 'math'. But an 'aftermath' is the grass which is cut after the first crop has been taken – in other words, a second crop of hay.

alarm

The Italian phrase, from which the word is derived, is quite dramatic:
All'arme, 'To arms!'

album

An *album* (from Latin *albus*, white) was, in ancient Rome, a blank, white
stone tablet on which public notices could be inscribed.

Its later meaning, a book with completely blank pages in which to insert
collected items, is first found in seventeenth-century Germany, where an
album amicorum was a blank book in which one's friends or fellow-scholars
could sign their names.

Today the term 'album' is used not only of the blank-leaved or 'white' book for
one's collection of autographs, stamps or photographs: through the notion of a
collection of things under one cover, it means, as commonly, a recording
containing a selection of musical hits by a particular group or artist.

alligator

When the Spaniards in the New World first saw alligators they were
astonished by their size. They called the creature *el lagarto*, the lizard – not
just any old lizard, but *the* lizard. When the name came into English, the
Spanish *el*, 'the', came with it; so, 'the alligator' is, strictly, 'the *THE* lizard'!

alyssum

This attractive little flower, frequently seen in rock-gardens or borders, was
once thought to be a cure for madness. This is the meaning that its name
literally conveys in Greek: it comes from *a-lyssa*, 'no madness'.

Amazon

Geographical names can have curious derivations, and one of the strangest
is that of the name of the river Amazon.

The Amazons, in Greek mythology, were a fabulous race of female warriors
in Scythia. They were huge and tough and used to cut off their right breasts
so that they could pull their bows back further.

The Greeks even explained the name, 'Amazon', as coming from the two
words, *a*, not, and *mazos*, a breast, so that an Amazon was a 'woman
without a breast'.

When Orellana, an early Spanish explorer, was sailing up a vast South
American river in 1541, he thought he saw some female warriors on the
banks. He immediately named the river the 'Amazon'.

amethyst

This blue quartz, much used in jewellery, was in former times prized not only
for its beauty but also for its supposed powers of preventing drunkenness.
Drinking cups made of amethyst were greatly valued in the ancient world.
The name comes from Greek *amethystos*, meaning 'not intoxicating', from *a*,
not, and *methyein*, to be drunk.

ammonia

This chemical has an unlikely derivation from the ancient Egyptian ram-headed God, Ammon.

There used to be a famous temple to Ammon in the Libyan oasis of Siwa, and it was near there that a salt of 'ammonia' was first found.

The fossils known as 'ammonites' also get their name from this ram-headed God, because they resemble a ram's horn in shape.

amok

A ferocious-sounding word, 'amok' or 'amuck' comes from Malay *amoq*, meaning 'rushing about in a murderous frenzy'.

For an English phrase comparable in meaning and power to 'running amok' we might turn to 'going berserk' (see ***berserk***), but this is equally foreign and bloodthirsty in origin.

amp

It seems rather unjust that, having achieved the distinction of being turned into a household word, one should suffer the misfortune of being cut in half – but this is what has happened to André Ampère, the French physicist and mathematician (1775-1836). His father suffered the same sad fate, rather more physically: he was guillotined in 1793, during the French Revolution.

An 'ampere', or 'amp' for short, is a unit of electric current, named after Ampère in recognition of his work on electricity.

ampersand

'Ampersand' is the name given to the sign '&', meaning 'and'. This sign used to follow on after the alphabet in old learning-books for children. The children would chant their alphabet through, and when they came to the sign '&' they would say "and, *per se*, and", meaning '&', on its own, means 'and'.

This, said quickly and clumsily, turned into 'ampersand'. (*Per se* is Latin for 'by itself'.)

Anthony

Should it be Anthony? or Antony? Why the two spellings? And where does the 'h' come from?

Properly speaking, Antony derives from the Roman name, Antonius, and has no 'h' in it. However, at the time of the Renaissance, when people were learning Greek, it was believed (wrongly, in fact) that the name came from the Greek word *anthos*, meaning 'flower'. We have the word in 'polyanthus' which means 'having many flowers' and in 'anthology' which is a collection of poetry or other writings, but means more literally 'a bunch of flowers'.

apple

Apple trees have been in Britain for as long as man can remember, and the name goes back into the distant past. The Old English word was *aeppel*; Old Norse was *epli*; Irish, *abhal*; Welsh, *Afal*; and modern German, *Apfel*.

Despite popular belief, the Bible does not mention 'apple' as a fruit with which the serpent tempted Adam and Eve. It is left without name.

But it is interesting to remember that in Latin *malum* means both 'apple' and 'evil'. There must have been some sort of linguistic link in the minds of the old monks as they illuminated their old Bibles.

April

This is thought to get its name from the Latin *aperire*, to open, because it is the month when the buds of flowers and trees open out. But there are other theories: one is that the word 'April' is connected with the name of the Greek goddess of love, Aphrodite – April being the time when young people traditionally turn their thoughts to love.

The Anglo-Saxons called the month *Easter-monath*, the month in which the dawn goddess Eastre had her festival.

FOOLS, FISH AND CUCKOOS!

The 'April Fool' custom is at least 400 years old. It's probably much older, but its origin is a mystery.

In France an April fool is called 'un poisson d'avril' – an 'April fish', and in Scotland he is called a 'gowk' – an old Norse word for a cuckoo.

arctic

A feeling of chill is conveyed by the very sound of 'arctic', but the word is not so bleak in its derivation. It comes from Greek *arktos*, bear, in this case the northern constellation of the Great Bear. The Pole Star, positioned over the North Pole, is in direct line with two stars in the Great Bear, and is itself in the constellation of the Little Bear.

arena

We must go back to the time of the gladiators to find the connection between the Latin word *arena*, which simply means 'sand', and the modern 'arena', a great sports enclosure for contests or displays.

At Rome the gladiatorial fights would take place in the amphitheatre, and sand was sprinkled over the ground to soak up the blood as fighters slashed at each other.

So, they were fighting on the 'sand-strewn place', or the *arena*.

Argentina

The Latin word *argentum*, silver, or money, passed into the Latin-based European languages: hence, French *argent*, and Italian *argento*. But in Spanish, the usual word for 'silver' was *plata*.

Spanish explorers of the sixteenth century found vast resources of silver in South America and supplies of it were transported down to the estuary that became known, because of this, as *Rio de la Plata*. However, when a federation of states was established in the area of the river, it was the Latin word for 'silver' that was preferred in forming its name – Argentina, or the 'Land of Silver'.

arrive

Literally, 'to arrive' means to come ashore, or, rather to reach the bank (French *rive*) of a river.

arrowroot

The arrowroot we put into desserts is a starch prepared from the root of the plant *Maranta arundinacea*, used in South America as an antidote to the poison with which arrows were tipped: it was applied to arrow-wounds to absorb the poison. Hence the name, you would think. But, although the form 'arrowroot' certainly reflects the plant's use in first-aid, the word may be, in origin, a corruption of its native name, *aru-aru*.

Ash Wednesday

Ash Wednesday is the first day of Lent. Traditionally this was the day when people began their period of fasting and repentance.

A thousand years ago or more, many people would rub themselves all over in ashes, and wear rough sacking, to demonstrate how sincerely they felt about being sorry for their sins. Later, priests would put ashes on sinners' heads. Gradually this died out and instead a symbolic cross was made on their foreheads in the ash produced from burning the palms which had been kept since the previous year's Palm Sunday. Some people still 'fast' during Lent, by going without sweets or cigarettes or something else which is a luxury.

aspidistra

Gracie Fields' music-hall song about 'The biggest aspidistra in the world' became so popular that the very word 'aspidistra' came to have a comical ring about it.

The shape of its leaves gives the plant its curious name. They are shaped something like shields - and the Greek word for 'shield' is *aspidos*.

assassin

'Assassin' comes from the Arabic plural term *hashshashin*, 'eaters of the drug hashish'. The *hashshashin* were a sect of Syrian Muslims who, under their sheikh (known picturesquely as the Old Man of the Mountains), conducted a campaign of terror against other Muslims at the time of the Crusades. The tradition is that they would drug themselves with hashish as a preparation for committing murder.

astronaut

Literally, the word 'astronaut' means 'star-sailer', from two Greek words, *astron*, star, and *nautes*, sailor.

This word, interestingly, is used chiefly of American spacemen. The Russians prefer the word 'cosmonaut'

Kosmos is Greek for universe – so Russian spacemen are 'universe-sailors'.

atlas

Atlas, according to the myth, was one of the ancient gods who made war upon Zeus. He was defeated, and as a punishment was condemned to bear heaven on his shoulders.

Older books of maps used to have a picture of Atlas on the cover – and so his name came to be given to any 'atlas'.

attic

You would hardly associate the dark, dusty, lumber-filled place below your roof with the glory of ancient Athens! Yet there is a strong link between the two places.

With a capital letter, 'Attic' means 'Athenian'. It comes from the word 'Attica', the name for the part of Greece in which Athens was situated.

When there was a revival of classical Greek styles of architecture during the seventeenth and eighteenth centuries, the name 'Attic storey' was given to the small, decorative, pillared storey sometimes added above a large classical façade.

The name passed to the space within a sloping roof – the space that we now think of as the 'attic'.

August

This month was named after the Roman emperor Augustus Caesar. He was actually born in September, but so many of his successes were achieved in August (or *Sextilis*, the 'sixth month', as it was previously called) that it was regarded as his special month. Also, it stood next to July, the month named after his great-uncle, Julius Caesar.

There is a tradition that Augustus insisted on having the same number of days in his month as July, and so he took one from February – this change being the last one to take place in Europe in a system of months that has remained unaltered for two thousand years.

The date of this final change was probably 8 BC. A proposal for a new World Calendar was presented to the United Nations in 1956 but found no favour, so it looks as if this Roman scheme will last a long while yet.

azalea

The name 'azalea' is taken from the Greek word *azaleos*, which means 'dry'.

The great classifier, Linnaeus, believed that the plant grew and flourished in dry soil.

baffle

This word goes back to the medieval days of chivalry, when, if a knight had done a dishonourable act he would be hung up by the heels, his scutcheon (shield with the family coat of arms) would be blotted, his spear would be broken, and he would be jeered at and insulted. Sometimes an effigy would be hung up instead. This process was known as being 'baffled'.

The word comes from the archaic French *beffler*, to mock.

barbecue

'Barbecue', a word that has recently grown in popularity with the increase of interest in outdoor parties and camping, has long been established in the US. In fact it comes from the West Indies, from Haiti, where *barbacòa* meant a wooden framework set up on posts. At one time in America it even meant a bedstead! Apparently the same sort of framework would do for sleeping on and for smoking meat on.

It came to mean the iron grid on which an animal could be roasted whole and, hence, the more sophisticated apparatus that descends from it.

The meaning 'an outdoor entertainment at which meat is roasted' has been around in the US for at least two hundred years.

bedlam

'Bedlam', of course, is noisy, disorganised chaos. It may come as a surprise, however, that the word is derived from 'Bethlehem'.

A famous London lunatic asylum was called 'Bethlehem Hospital' and in the eighteenth century it was a fashionable entertainment amongst ladies and gentlemen to go and watch the mad behaviour of the inmates.

The place was, indeed, 'bedlam'!

> ### BEDLAM – ENGLAND'S FIRST LUNATIC ASYLUM
>
> Founded in 1247 as the Priory of St. Mary Bethlehem, originally outside Bishopsgate in London. After the dissolution of the monasteries it was turned into a lunatic asylum in 1547.
>
> In *King Lear* Shakespeare writes:
>
> Of Bedlam beggars, who, with roaring voices.
> Strike in their numb'd and mortified bare arms
> Pins, wooden pricks, nailes, springs of rosemary . . .

bee

Bees are such familiar and universal insects that inevitably the name 'bee' stretches back into time immemorial. The Old English word was *beo*, and different forms of the word exist in Old High German and Old Norse.

They are attractive-looking creatures and have an enviable reputation for hard work and social harmony.

English girls are seldom if ever given the name 'Bee'. Nevertheless, the two first names, Melissa and Deborah both mean 'bee': – Melissa comes from the Greek, and Deborah from the Hebrew.

beetle

The word 'beetle' is linked with the word 'bite'. It comes from Old English *bitula*, meaning 'a thing that bites'.

beggar

You might well assume that a beggar is simply someone who begs. But it is more complicated than that. If you look up *bègue* in a French dictionary you will find it means 'stammerer'. What has this got to do with begging?

During the twelfth century, a certain Lambert le Bègue (Lambert the Stammerer) founded a religious order for women, who were called after him, in Latin, *beguinae* or *beghinae*. Some time later there grew up the equivalent male order, the *beghardi*. These *beguinae* and *beghardi* were lay nuns and monks: they took no vows and could return to the non-religious life when they chose. They were mendicants – that is, they went about asking for charity or 'begging'.

It is thought that *begard*, the Old French version of *beghardus*, gave us 'beggar' in English, and that the verb 'beg' came from 'beggar', rather than 'beggar' from 'beg'.

Modern French still has the word *béguine*, a lay nun.

belly

People tend to think of 'belly' as a very indelicate word. But it has an ancient and respectable history, and is surely preferable to the inaccurate 'stomach' or childish 'tummy'. It comes from Old English *baelg*, a bag. This, in turn, came from *belgan*, to swell.

Baelg also gives us 'bellows' – which is a sort of swelling bag.

berserk

This colourful word comes from Old Norse *berserkr*. A *berserkr* was a warrior whom the sight of a battle would fill with wild frenzy and furious fighting spirit. The name is thought to be made up of *bern*-, bear, and *serkr*, coat: warriors and champions liked to wear the skins of fierce animals

bikini
In 1946 the Bikini Atoll in the Pacific saw a series of what were then astonishingly powerful atom-bomb tests.

When the bikini swim-suit first appeared, a few months later, the effect on mankind was equally shattering. Hence the name.

biro®

The word 'biro', a common name for a ballpoint pen, comes from the name of the inventor of the ballpoint, Lázló Joseph Biró.

Born in Hungary, he began work on the ballpoint in his own country, but completed it in Argentina during the Second World War. Through the negotiations of his English backer, Henry Martin, the pen was accepted for use by the armed forces. This provided the boost it needed to sell on a wider market – so that the name 'biro' is now an everyday term in millions of households.

biscuit

Literally, this means 'twice cooked', from the two Latin words, *bis*, twice, and *coctus*, cooked. The earliest type of biscuit was *biscoctus (panis)*, twice-cooked bread, from which developed Old French *bescoit*, and modern French *biscuit* – the spelling used in English too. The word 'biscuit', as a pottery term, means porcelain that has had its first firing but is not yet glazed.

An interesting use of *bis*, twice, can be found in France. A French audience does not call *'Encore!'* for a piece to be performed a second time: it calls *'Bis!'*

bishop

What is the connection between a bishop and a microscope? In fact, they are fairly closely related, linguistically speaking.

A microscope (from Greek *mikros*, small), as we know, is a device for helping us to see small things; a telescope (Greek *tele*, far off) helps us to see distant things; a kaleidoscope (Greek *kalos*, beautiful, *eidos*, form) lets us see beautiful patterns of things. The 'scope' part comes from the Greek verb, *skopeein*, to see.

But what has this to do with a bishop? Well, the word 'bishop' is a version of the Greek word *episkopos*. *Skopos* is 'one who sees'; *epi* means 'over'; so an *episkopos* is an overseer – or someone who is in charge.

Black Maria

A 'Black Maria', of course, is the van in which police carry criminals to and from prison. It is a tough black security van. But who or what was Maria?

By all accounts Black Maria Lee was a huge negress who kept a lodging-house for seamen in Boston, USA, and she was famous for her massive size and toughness. Apparently, when the police were confronted by some specially awkward criminal, they used to send for 'Black Maria', who used to help them escort the baddies to prison. The name 'Black Maria' became famous and later, when vans came into use, it seemed an appropriate name for them.

blanket

Nowadays, of course, you can buy blankets of any colour, but in earlier times a blanket was a cover made of white wool.

The name 'blanket' comes from the French *blanc*, white, and was originally given to the white woollen cloth itself, from which clothes and covers were made. So a 'blanket' is simply 'a white cover'.

blitz

This word, a terrifying reminder of urban devastation and destruction was, before the Second World War, simply the German word for 'lightning'.

But the swift movement of Hitler's armoured divisions across Western Europe, backed by air strikes, earned the nickname *Blitzkrieg* or 'lightning war'. Shortened to 'blitz', the word was used in Britain of the intensive air-raids on London. Thus, in English, the word acquired a sinister new meaning that it had never had in German.

bloomers

A new-fangled costume of the mid-nineteenth century, long baggy trousers gathered in at the ankle and worn under a short skirt, was popularised by an American lady whose name forthwith passed into the English language. She was Mrs. Amelia Bloomer.

Mrs. Bloomer was a champion of women's rights and thought these trouser-like articles of clothing gave ladies more freedom. She died in 1894.

In the late nineteenth century a new style of 'bloomers' was invented – knee-length knickerbockers without the overskirt, which were intended to give women ease of movement for outdoor activities, especially cycling.

boggle

When does your mind 'boggle'? Strictly speaking, when it is scared stiff rather than merely astonished.

The word is linked with ghosts and the fear they arouse in us. It probably comes from Scots 'bogle', a hobgoblin or ghoul, which is one of the group of related words for frightening, supernatural creatures that also includes 'bogey', 'bugbear', Northern English 'boggart', and Welsh *bwg* (pronounced 'boog').

And students of Russian will probably be reminded that the Russian for God is *bog*.

bonfire

Why is it called a *bon*fire? Because, in origin, it is a *bone* fire, or the fire in which our ancestors used to burn their left-over scraps of animal bones.

bonsai

The name is Japanese and it is made up of two words: *bon*, meaning a tray or bowl, and *sai*, meaning cultivation.

It is something which is cultivated on a tray or in a bowl.

book

The earliest meaning of the word 'book' in Teutonic languages is believed to have been a 'wooden writing-tablet', on which letters known as runes were scratched. 'Book' is thought to have derived from an earlier form of the word 'beech' (this tree is *boc* in Anglo-Saxon) – a direct reminder of its wooden origin.

boss

We think of 'boss' as being very much an American word. In fact it has crossed the Atlantic twice.

It came originally from the Netherlands, where *baas* means 'master'. It accompanied the Dutch to America in the early days when New York was still called New Amsterdam, and also went with them to South Africa, where it still exists as *baas* in Afrikaans.

From the US it crossed back to Britain, as slang, and no doubt the American films of the 1920s helped to popularise it.

bowler hat

Bowler hats were originally made as a sort of crash-helmet to protect the head if you were thrown off your horse when hunting.

A Norfolk landowner asked a London hat-maker to design him a special hat for hunting, and this was eventually made, in 1850, by two brothers, Thomas and William Bowler, of Southwark. Their name has lived on ever since.

box

From the time of the Greeks and Romans, boxwood, being rather rare and expensive, was used for making small, delicate, lidded caskets for jewellery, ointments and other precious possessions.

The name 'box' for such a casket came from *pyxis*, the Latin word for a box made from boxwood.

It was not until as late as the eighteenth century that the word 'box' came to be used for larger containers for other purposes.

boycott

This word commemorates the name of Captain Charles Boycott, a land agent for an estate in County Mayo, Ireland, in the nineteenth century.

In 1880, discontented tenants, angry because of high rents and the Captain's refusal to discuss terms, decided to refuse to work for him, or to sell him goods, or to have any dealings with him whatever.

This treatment came to be known as 'boycotting'.

brand new

'Straight from the fire' – in other words it has just come from the smithy. The word, 'brand', is another form of 'burned'. In German there is a splendid word, *funkelnagelneu* which is literally 'spark nail new' and this also suggests an origin from the blacksmith's anvil.

BRAND NEW WORDS

The First Supplement to the Oxford English Dictionary (A-G) was published in 1972. It contained some surprisingly 'low' slang: bumf, burp, geezer, gimmick, grotty, git and gazump, just to list a few.

These may have been 'brand new' to the dictionary, but words often have to wait before they are given the dignity of being included in the dictionary.

No one knows where 'gimmick' came from: but 'bumf' is short for 'bum-fodder' (toilet paper); 'geezer' is a version of 'guiser' (an odd-looking old man); 'git' is a brat who is 'begotten'; and 'gazump' comes from the Yiddish 'gezumph', 'to swindle'.

The problem for dictionary-makers is to decide whether a word will continue to be used or whether it will just fade away.

Chambers Twentieth Century Dictionary, published in 1983, includes ra-ra skirt, total allergy syndrome, Space Invaders® and Harvey Smith salute.

Brazil

You might suppose that 'Brazil' is the native South American Indian name for the country, but this would be wrong.

Centuries before Brazil was ever discovered, the Romans had imported a red dye-wood from the East, which they called *brasilium*.

In the sixteenth century, when the Portuguese discovered, in their newly-acquired territory in South America, an abundance of trees producing a similar dye, they called the country *terra de brasil*, giving us the names Brazil (Brasil in Portuguese) and Brasília, the country's new capital city.

bren gun

Why *Bren*? Who was he? Or what is it?

The 'Br' comes in fact from the town of Brno, in the Czech Republic, where this type of gun was originally developed. And the 'en' part of the name comes from the town of Enfield, in Britain, where the gun was later manufactured.

Incidentally, the 'Sten' gun gets its name from the initials of the inventors (Shepherd and Turpin) and the 'en' was added to bring it into line with 'Bren' gun.

broker

When you 'broach' a topic in conversation you are 'opening it up'. This gives us a clue to the likely derivation of the word 'broker'.

A 'broker', originally, was a barman who used to 'open up' or 'broach' casks of wine with a spike called a 'broach' or 'broche'. (A 'brooch' being an object fastened with a spike or pin, is

another form of this word.)

'Broker', according to this theory, came to be used for dealers in commodities other than wine, and we find it in 'pawnbroker', 'stockbroker', etc.

The French use *broche* to mean both a brooch and a roasting-spit. And we have the architectural term 'broach-spire' for that

broom

This cheerful yellow flower has given its name to the longest line of kings in English history.

Count Geoffrey of Anjou, father of our King Henry II, used to wear a sprig of broom in is helmet. In Latin, the broom is *planta genista*, and this turned into the royal name, 'Plantagenet'.

Henry II came to the throne in 1154, and the last 'Plantagenet' king, Richard III, came to his sticky end at the Battle of Bosworth in 1485, almost 330 years later.

It is perhaps worth remembering that the twigs from 'broom' went to make besoms – hence the word for the long-handled sweeping brush is a 'broom'.

And years ago, the fields of broom in a hamlet near the area now known as Kensington in London, gave us the name 'Brompton' or 'Broom town'. Today we still have Brompton Road, and the Brompton Oratory.

budgerigar

This is Australian. It is made up of two aboriginal words: *budgeri*, meaning 'good', and *gar*, which means 'cockatoo'. So, a budgerigar is simply 'a good cockatoo'.

Incidentally, 'cockatoo' comes from Malay *kakatua*.

budget

The word 'budget' goes back centuries. In early times it used to mean a large leather bag. When the Chancellor of the Exchequer revealed his plans, people used to say that he was 'opening his budget' – in other words, he was taking his plans out of his bag. And after a while, the plans themselves came to be called the 'budget'.

When we see the Chancellor holding up his red dispatch-box at the door of No. 11 Downing Street, what we are looking at is our version of the old 'bougette' or leather bag.

bug

There is something nasty about the word 'bug' – far worse than 'insect'.

It may be linked with the Welsh word *bwg*, a hobgoblin, and with our own word *bugbear*, which means an object of terror.

The word 'bogey' and 'bogeyman' are probably also linked with 'bug'. It is worth making a comparison with the word *larva*, too. (See *larva*)

bunk or bunkum

The county of Buncombe in North Carolina has its place in linguistic history because once its member in Congress talked such lengthy twaddle that he was taken to task for wasting time.

His reply that he must "make a speech for Buncombe", gave the language the pithily dismissive word 'bunkum', and its shortening, 'bunk'.

Perhaps the most famous use of the latter is in Henry Ford's memorable sneer: "History is bunk".

bureaucracy

This word has a long and complicated history. The Latin *burrus* means 'red' and from this came Old French *burel*, the name of a woollen cloth, presumably originally reddish in colour. Desks were often covered with this kind of cloth, and came to be called *bureaux* because of their covering. The word 'bureau' developed further, to mean an office, and then even the occupants of the office. Finally, with *-cracy* added (Greek *kratos* means 'power'), we have 'bureaucracy' – government by officials.

bus

'Bus' is now, of course, a word in its own right, but it is worth remembering that it is actually the last syllable of the Latin word, *omnibus*, which means 'with everybody'.

The word 'omnibus' was first used for a public vehicle in Paris in 1828, and in 1829 a similar vehicle started a public service in London.

For years people felt that the proper word was 'omnibus' and always put an apostrophe before the 'b' when they wrote 'bus. But this practice has almost entirely disappeared now.

butcher

Believe it nor not, the word 'butcher' comes from Old French *bochier*, which means 'a slaughterer of he-goats'! *Boc* was the Old French and Provençal word for 'he-goat'. The English word 'buck' is connected with it.

buttercup

At one time it was thought that buttercups were especially good for increasing the butter content of milk. In fact, the yellow colour of butter was supposed to be a result of the cows eating 'butter'cups.

calculator

Possibly no word demonstrates the march of technology more than this one! The Latin *calculus*, from which it comes, means 'a small stone' or 'pebble': pebbles were used in antiquity for counting or reckoning.

Thus the word 'calculator' has a history stretching back for more than two thousand years, and marks the progress from stones to electronics.

camera

In modern Italian, *camera* is simply 'a room'. In Latin it was a vault. Greek *kamara* could be any of several things with an arched cover or top, including a vaulted chamber.

The modern use of 'camera' comes from the term *camera obscura*, 'a dark room'.

canary

Canaries, of course, are named after the Canary Islands. But why were the Canary Islands given this name? Oddly enough because of the *dogs* that were found there. The Latin for dog is *canis*, and the Romans called the largest of the islands 'Canaria'. So there is a curious linguistic connection between the words 'canine' and 'canary'!

candidate

Candidatus, the Latin word from which this comes, originally meant 'clothed in white'. All who offered themselves for positions of public service in ancient Rome were dressed in white. *Candidus* is Latin for 'white'.
White being the colour of truth and purity, *candidus* developed to mean 'honest' and 'frank', the meanings also conveyed by English 'candid'.

candytuft

This little plant, with its flowers in 'tufts', makes a pretty border decoration. But why the 'candy'?

Quite simply, it was originally imported from Crete – and an earlier name for this Mediterranean island was *Candia*. It is a tufted plant from Crete.

canter

This takes us back to the times of Geoffrey Chaucer and the pilgrims who used to go to Canterbury. 'Canter' is short for 'Canterbury gallop', the easy pace of those going to the famous shrine of St. Thomas à Becket.

Canterbury bell

Pilgrims visiting various shrines in the Middle Ages would buy distinctive mementos from the places they had seen. A scallop shell, for example, worn as a badge, would signify a visit to the shrine of St. James at Compostela in Northern Spain. Visitors to Canterbury would buy little tinkling bells for their horses to wear, and the flower, looking like one of these, is called after this pilgrim's souvenir.

CANTUAR AND EBOR

Bishops of the Church of England officially sign their names with their Christian names followed by the Latin equivalent of their sees (dioceses).

Thus the Archbishop of Canterbury signs himself George Cantuar, and the Archbishop of York signs himself John Ebor (the Latin name for York was Eboracum)

---

capricious

Goats or hedgehogs? Surprisingly the latter!

To be 'capricious' means to be unpredictable, inconstant, and led by fancy. A sudden whim or change of mind is called a 'caprice' and the musical term 'capriccio' is used to mean a lively, unconventional piece.

The English words are derived, in fact, from Italian *capriccio*, which has a rather strange history. It now means 'a whim' but used to mean 'a shudder', having developed from Latin *caput*, head, and *ericius*, hedgehog, to convey the notion of 'a head with hair standing on end'. The modern meaning of *capriccio* came from a mistaken association with the word *capro*, a goat (from Latin *caper*). Certainly it is the idea of wild, goatlike jumping about that is behind the meanings of 'caprice' and 'capricious' in English.

Latin *caper* can be rather more genuinely spotted in the name of the zodiac symbol 'Capricorn', and in the kind of 'caper' that you cut.

Capricorn

Those who have birthdays between 22 December and 20 January will probably know that they are born under the zodiac sign of Capricorn. The name 'Capricorn' comes from two Latin words: *caper*, 'goat', and *cornu*, 'horn'. So, 'Capricorn' really means a 'horned goat'.

If you are capricious, or full of caprice, it means you are, like a goat, very changeable and likely to jump from one idea to another. And if you caper about, this also means that you leap around like a goat. Even the musical term, 'capriccio' comes from the same Latin word.

Yet more surprising, our word 'cab', as in 'taxi-cab' also derives from this 'goat-word'. The French 'cabriolet', a one-horse carriage, got its name from the Italian *capriole*, because it was so light and speedy – unlike previous coaches. And 'cab' is simply short for 'cabriolet'.

Finally, if you ever fly from Gatwick, perhaps you'll like to remember that this village gained its name from being a Saxon 'goat-farm', or 'gat-wick'.

car

The origin of this common word is the Latin *carrus*, which was a two-wheeled cart.
The strange fact is, however, that in English the word 'car' came to be used as a rather flowery poetical term for an elaborate triumphal chariot. More mundanely, it has been used for various types of truck, carriage and railway wagon.
Some people still like to refer to the vehicle propelled by internal combustion rather precisely as a 'motor-car'.

carat

When you talk of a 'nine-carat' gold ring, you are referring to the actual fineness of the gold: twenty-four carat gold is pure gold, and nine-carat gold has only nine twenty-fourths of gold in it.

The strange name for this measurement derives from the Arabic *qirat* meaning the seed of the Carob-tree. Such tiny seeds were once used as weights.

cardigan

Named after James Thomas Brudenell, seventh Earl of Cardigan (1797-1868), the soldier who led the Charge of the Light Brigade at Balaclava in 1854. He is said to have worn a knitted 'over-waistcoat', a garment which quickly gained popularity in the army during the winters of the Crimean campaign.

cardinal

The important 'princes' of the Roman Catholic Church are called 'cardinals', and from among themselves they choose who will be Pope. But why are they called 'cardinals'?

The word comes from the Latin *cardines* which, surprisingly, means 'hinges'. In ecclesiastical use, the Latin word *cardinalis* was originally an adjective applied to the priests and bishops attached as principals (or 'hinges') to a particular church. The word grew in prestige as it became used as a noun and restricted to the clergy who were the *cardinales* or 'hinge-men' of the Church of Rome.

carnation

'Carnation' formerly meant 'flesh colour', from Latin *carnatio*, fleshiness. The flower is generally thought to have got its name from its pink or crimson colour. But there is the puzzling fact that this flower was once also called 'coronation' (from latin *corona*, crown), maybe because it was used in wreaths for the head. Whichever was the original form, the two words became confused, and the flower has been 'carnation' ever since 1600.

carnival

The origin of this cheerful word is very odd indeed. Literally, it means 'putting meat away from you'!

In medieval times people used to fast during Lent, and just before they did this they had a grand celebration of eating and merriment. After these festivities they 'put meat away' – but the festivities themselves took on the name 'carnival'.

The word is thought to derive from Latin *carnem levare* (*caro*, flesh, *levare*, to remove) giving medieval Latin *carne-levarium*, the early form of 'carnival'.

carol

Originally this was a dance accompanied by song; the word comes from Provençal *carola*, a ring-dance. The derivation of this Provençal word is disputed, but it may come from Latin *corolla*, a little garland, or *choraula*, a flautist accompanying a chorus.

Carols were, by the fourteenth century, popular religious songs, and it would appear that the majority dealt with Christmas themes. So the association of carols with Christmas is a strong and old-established one.

caterpillar

An odd name for a curious-looking creature. How did it come by it?

Literally it means a 'hairy cat', being derived from two Latin words: *catta*, cat and *pilosus*, hairy.

Norman French had the word *chatepelose*, thought to be the direct origin of 'caterpillar'. The usual French term for 'caterpillar' is *chenille*, from Latin *canicula*, a little *dog*!

cathedral

When is a large church called a 'cathedral'?

When a bishop has his throne or 'seat' there. *Kathedra* is Greek for 'seat'.

Catherine wheel

This firework is a reminder of the cruel death suffered by St. Catherine of Alexandria, who refused to betray the name of Christ, and who was therefore tied to a huge spiked wheel and tortured. The legend says that God sent a fire from heaven and broke the wheel in pieces. But her tormentors beat her instead and beheaded her.

chaffinch

As it scavenges around hayricks and apparently likes to enjoy pecking around in chaff, this particular finch gets the name chaffinch. The 'finch' part of the name is Old English, *finc*.

cenotaph

This comes from Greek *kenotaphion*, which is made up of two words: *kenos*, empty, and *taphos*, tomb. So it means an 'empty tomb'. Cenotaphs, as is the case with the one in Whitehall at which the Queen lays a wreath on Remembrance Day, are not really tombs, but memorials to those buried elsewhere. By contrast, the Tomb of the Unknown Soldier in Westminster Abbey contains an anonymous body.

chap

This word has hovered about in the language for several centuries – never quite gaining respectability as a 'proper' word, and yet not really very slangy.

It is actually an abbreviation of a longer word, the archaic 'chapman', meaning a merchant or trader, which is itself etymologically linked with 'cheap'.

'Chap' in the sixteenth century meant a 'customer' or 'purchaser', but had taken on the meaning 'fellow' by the early eighteenth century.

chapel

The story goes that St. Martin, Bishop of Tours, when he was serving as a young man with the Roman army, met a naked beggar one cold winter's day. He was so sorry for him that he took his own cloak, cut it in half with his sword, and gave one half to the beggarman.

Later, when he had been made a saint, his cloak was kept as a sacred relic in a special sanctuary.

The medieval Latin name for 'cloak', *cappella*, passed to the sanctuary, and it is from this word that 'chapel' is derived.

For many years the 'cappella' of St. Martin was France's most holy relic, and was carried as a banner to ensure victory in war. The keeper of this was called the *chapelain:* and this has given us the English word 'chaplain'.

chauvinist

'Male chauvinist pig' is a modern term of abuse (or proud label) reserved for men who refuse to allow women their equal rights. It may be forgotten that the word 'chauvinist' used to mean someone exaggeratedly loyal to his country. It comes from the name of Nicholas Chauvin, a soldier in the French army, whose fanatical devotion to Napoleon made him something of an absurdity.

checkmate

The game of chess has been played for well over a thousand years. It was probably invented in India, whence it spread to Persia, so that many of the terms used in the game are of Indian or Persian origin.

'Check' comes, via Old French *eschec*, from Persian *shah*, king; 'checkmate' is from the Persian phrase *shah mat*, meaning 'the king is dead'.

cheers!

We might be surprised, as we down a pint at the pub with the exclamation 'Cheers!', to learn of the journey that the word has made down the centuries from its unexpected origin, the Late Latin word *cara*, face.

Cara turned into Old French *chiere* or *chere*, which passed into English, still with the meaning 'face': as late as 1590 we find Helena, in Shakespeare's *Midsummer Night's Dream* (III, 2, 96), ''pale of cheere''.

From the idea of 'face' developed the meaning 'facial expression', then 'mood' – a sense reflected in the phrase 'be of good cheer'. Food and other good things that produce a 'cheerful' face came to be called 'cheer', too.

A 'cheer', as a shout of encouragement, was known two hundred years ago; but the custom of raising a glass with the shout 'Cheers!' seems to be of twentieth-century origin. And of even more recent development is the use of 'Cheers!' to mean 'Thank you!'

chess

If you look up the French for 'chess', you will find that it is a plural term, *échecs*, literally, 'checks'. The Old French form of this plural, *esches*, is the word from which the English word 'chess' is derived. Its singular, *eschec*, is, as mentioned under **checkmate**, from Persian *shah*, king.

The name 'chess' can therefore be interpreted as 'the game of kings'.

chestnut

The name has nothing at all to do with chests. 'Chestnut' trees are so called because the name derives from the Latin *castanea*, which in turn may be from *Castana*, in Thessaly. (See **horse chestnut**)

Christmas

The word 'Christmas' is readily analysed as the *Mass* (in this case in the sense 'festival') of the birth of *Christ*. But where does the word 'Mass' come from?

The English word developed from its Latin form *missa*. But there is controversy over the origin of *missa*. The most popular theory is that it comes from the phrase *Ite, missa est* (perhaps short for *Ite, missa est contio*, 'Go, the congregation is dismissed'), used at the end of the Latin service.

choleric

Meaning 'bad-tempered' or 'irascible', this word reflects the old idea that a mixture of fluids or 'humours' in your body was responsible for your character. One of these 'humours' was bile or 'choler' (associated with the Greek word for bile, *chole*) – an excess of which would incline you to lose your temper easily. (See **humour**)

chrysalis

The Greek word for 'gold' is *chrysos*. A 'chrysalis' originally meant a 'gold-coloured' butterfly pupa. Of course, they are not all golden-coloured, but the word still suggests the beauty of gold.

it's a cinch!

But what is a cinch?

It is a saddle-girth used in Mexico, noted for its firmness. The Mexicans got the word *cincha* from the Spaniards, and they, in turn, got it from the Latin *cingula*, belt.

Cinderella's glass slipper

The story of Cinderella is such a fairy-tale fantasy that we almost overlook the absurdity of the 'glass' slipper.

However, in French there is a confusion of *vair*, meaning 'fur' and *verre*, meaning 'glass'. It could well be a misunderstanding of spelling or a mix-up of the two similar-sounding words which has given us this strange slipper made of 'glass'.

climax

We use the word 'climax' in a variety of ways to suggest a summit of experience: a culmination, a final point of ecstasy.

In fact, it is a Greek word with a much more practical meaning: to the Greeks a *climax* was simply a 'ladder'.

cloche

We call cloches after their shape – 'bell'-shape. It is simply the French word for a bell, used in a different context.

Old-style 'cloches' were in fact bell-shaped, and only later did the different modern styles develop.

Our word 'clock' comes from the same source, having, as many 'clocks' do, a bell. And the German word *Glocke* also means a 'bell', as we can see in the musical instrument *Glockenspiel*.

Bells, clocks, cloches: they are all the same. *(see **xylophone**)*

clue

With detectives from Sherlock Holmes onwards looking everywhere for 'clues', the original meaning of 'clue' has become obscured. It was, especially with the alternative spelling 'clew', 'a ball of thread'!

How did the word come to have its present meaning?

The answer lies in the story of Theseus and the Minotaur of Crete, who lived in a maze. Theseus took a ball or 'clew' of thread into the maze with him, unravelling it as he went, and when he had killed the monster he had a 'clue' to how to get out again.

cobra

If ever you have seen a cobra about to attack, you will remember the amazing hood which it swells up around its neck. The full name of this snake is *cobra de capello*, which is Portuguese for 'snake of the hood'.

The Portuguese got their word *cobra* from the earlier Latin word *coluber*, which simply meant 'a snake'. Nowadays, zoologists in fact use a variation of that word for a whole genus of snakes, the Colubridae, which form the largest family of snakes.

cobweb

The 'web' part is obvious: weavers were once webbers and a 'web' is something that is woven. But what about the 'cob'?

A Saxon word which we have almost completely forgotten is the strange-looking *attercop*, meaning a spider. So the 'cobweb' was once called a 'copweb', which was short for an attercop's web.

'Attor' meant poison; and 'coppa' meant either a round head or else a cup. 'Attor' could also refer to a venomous malignant person. The point was that spiders were supposed to be poisonous.

In his translation of the Bible, Wycliffe translated Isaiah lix, as 'the webbis of an attercop' – which becomes 'the spider's

cockchafer

The maybug. The word 'chafer' or 'chaffer' is a dialect term for a beetle.

The 'cock' part of the name may refer to their relatively large size, but it could also refer to a former practice of making these insects fight. (See *maybug*)

coconut

Next time you see a coconut on a fruit-stall, look at it carefully. The three black marks at one end of it look like the eyes and mouth in a brown, hairy, ugly face.

Unlikely as it may seem, this is how coconuts get their name! *Coco* is Portuguese and Spanish for an 'ugly face', or 'bogey-man'.

codeine

This is an alkaloid obtained from opium, and it is a useful analgesic and sedative. Its name is derived from the Greek word for a poppy-head – *kodeia*.

colonel

An oddly-spelt word, seeing that we pronounce it 'kurnel'.

The reason is that a colonel was the leader of a column of soldiers – and the Latin for column is *colonna*. The pronunciation has changed, to make it easier for English tongues to say it.

conkers

Everyone knows the game of conkers, much enjoyed by children in the autumn.

The name 'conker' is interesting. It is associated with 'conquerors', but it is quite likely to have its origins in a similar game which used to be played with snail shells, and the dialect name for these snail shells was 'conker'.

Going back to the origin of snail shell 'conkers' takes us to the Latin *concha*, shell, which in turn derives from the Greek word *kogkhe*, meaning mussel – a far cry from horse chestnut trees!

No child could have played with conkers before the reign of James I, as the horse chestnut did not arrive in this country until 1600. (See *chestnut* and *horse chestnut*)

companion

The middle section of this word is interesting in that it comes from the Latin for 'bread' – *panis*. A 'companion' is literally someone you share your bread with.

complexion

Nowadays we use this word to mean the general appearance and state of the skin, especially that of the face.

In the Middle Ages, however, the word had a strangely different meaning. Doctors thought that in your body there was a mixture of 'humours' and that your character was determined by the proportions in which these were present inside you.

Your 'complexion' from Latin *complectere* (in its literal meaning, 'to plait together'), was your own particular intermixture of 'humours'.

The colour of a person's face was an important clue to his 'complexion' or temperament, so the meaning of 'complexion' changed gradually from the mixture within the body to the outward appearance of the skin.

(See *humour*)

conspiracy

The Latin word *spirare* meant 'to breathe', and so 'inspire' means 'to breath in', 'expire' means 'to breathe out'; and 'conspire' literally means 'to breathe together'.

Just imagine a group of 'conspirators' with their heads together, breathing the same air.

copper

This metal gets its name from the place where, in antiquity, it was chiefly mined – Cyprus. The Latin *cuprum*, 'copper', comes from the term *Cyprium aes*, 'Cyprian metal'.

cor blimey!

A weird expression that might well mystify a foreigner – but perhaps most of us remember being told at some time that it is a distorted version of an odd exclamatory oath, 'God blind me!'

corporal

Just as a colonel leads a *column* of men, so a corporal leads a *body* of men. Latin for a body is *corpus*, and this gives us quite a number of English words: corpse – a dead body; corps – a body of military men; corporal punishment – hurting the body; corporation – an official body of people; corpulent – having a fat body; and even a blood corpuscle is a tiny 'body' in the blood. There are colleges in both Oxford and Cambridge called Corpus Christi – and these are founded in honour of the 'Body of Christ': and this, of course, means the bread of the Communion Service.

So, one way or another, *corpus* is very much a part of our Latin word-borrowing into English.

cosh

This word has a history as a slang or dialect term for a stick, especially 'the cane' at school, or the police 'truncheon'. Some say it is a word from Romany, the language of the gypsies, and comes from *koshter*, meaning 'stick'.

country

'Country' is derived from Latin *contra*, 'opposite' or 'against' (the word that also gives us 'contrary'), through the notion of a tract of landscape laid out in front of, or opposite, the observer.

An attractive theory suggests that 'country-dance' has nothing to do with 'country', but is derived from French *contre-danse*, a dance in which partners stand *contre* or 'opposite' each other; but apparently the truth is that the French adopted the English term 'country-dance' and converted it to *contre-danse* through a mistaken association of the word with the position of the dancers.

cowslip

A pretty name for a charming countryside flower, you may think. But it is actually somewhat repulsive. The 'slip' comes from Old English *slyppe*, slime. The name is thought to mean 'cow-dung'!

cravat

Croat mercenary soldiers used to wear a sort of linen necktie, and this was copied by the French in the seventeenth century, during the Thirty Years War. The French name for the Croats was *Cravates*, and the name was adopted for the necktie.

cream

Though you would not link Jesus Christ with cream, 'Christ' and 'cream' both derive from Greek *chriein*, to anoint.

Ecclesiastical Latin *chrisma* ('chrism' in English), the holy oil made of spices and olive oil used in anointing ceremonies, developed into Old French *cresme*, the word from which 'cream' came.

'Christ' comes from *christos*, the past participle of *chriein*, and means 'the Anointed One'.

creosote

This word, oddly, means 'flesh-preserver', from the Greek words, *kreas*, flesh, and *soter*, saviour.

The name was originally given to a liquid produced from wood-tar, which has antiseptic qualities and was used in medical treatment.

The oily liquid with the same name, bought at the ironmonger's, is made from coal-tar – and of course we use it to preserve wood rather than flesh.

cretin

This has come to mean 'idiot', but in origin it is just a Swiss-French version of 'Christian'!

Crestin (which became French *crétin* and English 'cretin') was the local term for certain people of the Valais district of Switzerland who were physically deformed and mentally defective as a result of congenital thyroid deficiency.

A common enough meaning of 'Christian' used to be 'human being' – and this was all that *crestin* meant. These people, though so deformed, were still 'humans'.

crikey!

Just as 'Gosh!' avoids saying 'God!', so 'Crikey!' avoids saying 'Christ!' And several other words hint at Christ, without actually using his name: for example, 'Crumbs!', 'Cripes!' and even 'For crying out loud!'

Then there are a number of Jesus-avoiding words such as 'Gee whizz!', and then again, other expressions such as 'Jiminy Cricket!' and 'Jeepers creepers!' that avoid saying 'Jesus Christ!'

crinoline

The name of this elegant nineteenth-century petticoat becomes disappointingly unromantic if you analyse it. 'Crinoline' was originally the fabric used for petticoats – linen stiffened with horse-hair, from Latin *crinis*, hair, and *linum*, flax.

criss-cross

'Criss-cross' was originally 'Christ-cross'. This was a name for the Maltese cross, a stylised representation of Christ's cross, that was placed before the alphabet in old learning-books for children. 'Criss-cross' even became a synonym for 'alphabet' but by the nineteenth century, the word was being regarded merely as a reduplication or intensified form of 'cross' – something like 'mishmash' or 'zigzag'.

crystal

It was an ancient belief that lumps of crystal were formed from pieces of ice which had become so hardened over the centuries that they could never be melted again.

The name, crystal, is a reminder of this notion, for it comes straight from the Greek word for 'ice', *krystallos*.

currant

Currants, little dried-up wizened grapes from the eastern Mediterranean, are called after the place from which they were first exported – Corinth.

In Old French they were called *raisins de Corinthe*, and in Middle English *raysons of Coraunce*. This rather long name became reduced to *Coraunce*, whose variant forms *corans* and *currans* were taken as plurals. The singular 'currant' appears in the seventeenth century.

cushy

'Cushy' arises from a combination of two Hindustani words, *khush*, pleasant, and *khushi*, pleasure, which derive from Persian. It came into our language from soldiers who served in India and brought it back to Britain as a part of their army slang.

czar

It can be too easily taken for granted that the 'Czar' of Russia is a title which is purely Russian.

But the long line of Russian Czars got their name through an early version of German *kaiser*, emperor, from the family name of the first Roman emperors, Caesar.

dachshund

Dachs is German for 'badger', so a *Dachshund* is a 'badger-dog'. It was bred for use in badger-hunting, as its long, low shape was ideal for going down into the badger sets, where it would bark frantically, without actually attacking the badger, till the hunters caught up with it.

daisy

As is well known, the daisy is very sensitive to sunlight; it opens in the morning and closes at night or in wet weather.

Since it opens and closes like an eye, it earned the name 'day's eye' (Old English *daeges eage*), which became 'daisy'. The name is hundreds of years old. Chaucer, in the *Legend of Good Women*, comments:

"Wele (well) by reson men it calle may

The dayeseye or ellis (else) the eye of day".

dandelion

How did the plant get this curious name?

It comes from French *dent de lion*, 'lion's tooth'. Its German name *Löwenzahn* has exactly the same meaning. Certainly it takes some imagination to see a lion's tooth in the shape of the leaf, usually understood to be the source of the name. Another possibility is that it comes from the long white pointed root.

As the name is French, you might suppose that it is used in France, too: but if you look up the French for 'dandelion', and work out its meaning, you'll get a rude shock, for it is *pissenlit*. Search further, and you'll find that an older English name for it is 'piss-a-bed'. These names come from the plant's diuretic properties.

dauphin

This name, used until the last century for the French heir to the throne, means literally 'dolphin'.

Dolphins have been noted since ancient times for their friendliness towards human beings: "Of a man he is nothing afraid . . . but meeteth their ships, plaieth and disporteth himselfe and fetcheth a thousand friskes and gambols before them", says the Roman writer Pliny, according to Philemon Holland's translation of 1601.

The word 'dolphin' comes from the Greek *delphis*, which became *delphinus*, in Latin. Perhaps because of the attractive character of the animal, 'Dolphin' became used as a Christian name; in its Latin form *Delphinus* or French form *Dauphin*, it was borne so traditionally by the counts of Vennois in south-eastern France that it came to be regarded as their family name and was finally assumed as a title.

Guigues IV of Vennois is thought to have been the first to use 'Dauphin' as a title and he had a dolphin as his distinctive heraldic device. The land he ruled was called Dauphiné.

A later count, Humbert II, whose own son had died, sold his lands in 1349 to Charles de Valois, the future Charles V of France. As Charles now had possession of Dauphiné, he assumed the title 'Dauphin', but when he actually succeeded to the throne, in 1364, he gave the title to his son.

The title lasted almost five hundred years, until 1830, when the Duc d'Angoulême, son of Charles X, renounced it.

December

At one time the Romans began their calendar in March, and had only ten months in the year. That made December the *tenth* month, from Latin *decem*, ten.

deck-chair

The name comes from the chairs that are on the 'deck' of a ship: but what, then, is a 'deck'.

Basically, it means a 'cover', linked with the Dutch word *dekken*, to cover, and also the Middle Dutch word *dec*, a 'roof'. So a ship's deck is the cover over the hold.

It is easy to see the connection with the phrase to 'deck oneself up' with finery – it is then that we 'cover' ourselves.

delirious

You are said to be 'delirious' when your mind is wandering, for instance when you are seriously ill with fever. Literally, however, you are 'wandering from the furrow'. The Latin word *lira* means 'furrow', so 'de-lirious' comes from an image of erratic steering in ploughing!

delphinium

Look carefully at the projection (or nectary) at the back of these flowers and if you can imagine it looks something like a dolphin, then you are seeing what the Greeks saw when they named the flower. The Greek word *delphinion* means 'a little dolphin'.

derrick

Thomas Derrick, who lived from the end of the sixteenth century well into the seventeenth, was one of England's more famous hangmen. He pursued his lethal trade for almost half a century and his name became a byword for death by the gibbet. Among the hundreds of people he hanged during his professional career was Robert Earl of Essex in 1601. Because the crane (originally the kind used on board ship) resembled a gibbet, it became nicknamed a 'derrick', now an established item of technical vocabulary, but with a rather sinister past.

devil

The French version of this word, *diable*, and the adjective 'diabolic', give a better clue than 'devil' itself does, to its derivation.

Green *diabolos* means 'accuser' or 'slanderer', and the adjective *diabolikos* means 'slanderous'. They come from the two words, *dia*, across and *ballein*, to throw. You could say that something 'diabolic' is 'thrown across' your path!

Through the idea that a 'slanderer' is an 'enemy', *diabolos* came into Christian use as a name for the Enemy, Satan, and from it eventually came Italian *diavolo*, Spanish *diablo*, French *diable*, German *Teufel* and English 'devil'.

What the dickens!

As you may well suspect, the word 'Dickens' in the expression 'What the Dickens!' has nothing whatever to do with the author of *Oliver Twist*.

Just as people have avoided actual blasphemy by using 'Gosh!', 'Crikey!' and 'Jeepers Creepers!' in place of 'God!', 'Christ!' and 'Jesus Christ!', so 'the Dickens!' was used as a substitute for 'the Devil!' There may be some connection with the names Dick or Dickon, pet-forms of Richard, but this is uncertain.

But it has also been suggested that 'Dickens' is a corrupted version of 'devilkin', a little devil; 'devilkin' turned into 'de'ilkin' which became 'dickin' and eventually 'dickens'.

Shakespeare, writing more than two hundred years before the birth of Charles Dickens, puts into the mouth of Mistress Page the words "I cannot tell what the dickens his name is!" (*Merry Wives of Windsor* III, 2, 19).

diddle

Back in 1803 a play called *Raising the Wind* came out, written by James Kenney. In it there was a cheat and rogue called Jeremy Diddler. The play was popular and this character's name gave us 'diddle', to cheat or swindle, a word that has long outlived any memories of the character, the play, or its author.

digit

One of the easiest and most natural ways to count is simply to use your fingers.

Latin for a finger is *digitus*, and the word 'digit' is directly derived from the use of fingers in making simple calculations. (see **calculus**)

dinosaur

The word dinosaur is made up of two Greek words: *deinos*, terrible, and *sauros*, lizard. It is, therefore, a 'terrible lizard'.

This is an example of the way scientists have used ancient Greek words for modern discoveries – for 'dinosaurs' were not known about until their remains were dug up in the nineteenth century. The name had to be invented.

diplomatic

'Diploma' comes from a Greek word meaning 'a folded piece of paper'. A 'diplomat' is literally someone who deals with these folded bits of paper. In other words he is skilled in negotiating and avoids awkward moments by keeping his documents 'diplomatically' folded over.

disaster

This word reflects people's belief in the influence of the stars. It comes (through French *désastre* or Italian *disastro*, both meaning 'calamity') from Latin *astrum*, star, with the negative prefix *dis-*: a 'dis-astrum' is an occasion when the stars are unfavourable.

disgusting

If unpleasant things are disgusting, shouldn't pleasant things be gusting? Well, perhaps!

Gustus is Latin for 'taste', so that if something is *dis*-gusting it simply means that it takes your taste away and puts you off your food.

Incidentally, the Italian word, *gusto* means precisely the same, so that when you do something 'with gusto' you are very pleased, and 'enjoying the taste'.

disco

In origin this is an abbreviation of 'discothèque' - a word coined by the French as a cross between *disque*, a record, and *bibliothèque*, a library.

In the 1940s, a 'discothèque' was just a 'record-library', but in the '50s the name was applied to shops selling records, and then to cafés or bars where customers could select records to dance to. The modern use, a night club or party with dancing to recorded music, became common in the '60s.

But, looking farther back, we find the Latin word *discus* (from Greek *diskos*), a 'plate', or 'quoit', which has given us many separate descendent words, all meaning something flat: not only 'disc' and 'disk', but also 'dish', 'discus', 'desk' and 'dais'; and through *disque*, the French version of 'disc', the modern 'disco'.

dismal

A useful synonym to 'gloomy' or 'dreary', 'dismal' is strangely derived. It was originally a noun, meaning 'unlucky days', from Latin *dies mali*. These were, in the medieval calendar, the two unpropitious days in each month. Also known as 'Egyptian days", they had been calculated by Egyptian astrologers, or were related to the occurrences of the plagues of Egypt described in the Bible.

There were, however, several sets of 'unlucky days', and John Aubrey in his *Miscellanies* notes all the lucky and unlucky days of the Jews, Greeks and Romans. After the Reformation the *dies mali* lost much of their importance. Apart from the word 'dismal' itself, little remains from this mass of superstition beyond the widespread dread of 'Friday the thirteenth'.

doh ray me fah soh lah te doh

These weird syllables will be immediately recognisable to singers and musicians as the notes of the scale in the Tonic Sol-fa notation scheme.

Anyone who has seen *The Sound of Music* will remember the song "Doe, a Deer", which was no more than a punning attempt to give some sort of meaning to these apparently arbitrary and nonsensical sounds. Where did they really come from?

Guido of Arezzo, also known as Aretino, a musical theorist who died in 1050, was their originator. There was a Latin hymn to St. John the Baptist by Paulus Diaconus, in which the opening syllables of each line happened to fall in turn on the rising notes of the hexachord (Guido's six-note scale), enabling him to use them as a guide in teaching singing. The Latin hymn goes like this:

Ut queant laxis
*Re*sonare fibris
*Mi*ra gestorum
*Fa*muli tuorum
*Sol*ve polluti
*La*bii reatum . . .

This gives us 'ut', 're', 'mi', 'fa', 'sol', 'la'. 'Si' (taken from *Sancte Ioannes*, the last line of the hymn, and later changed to 'te') was added sometime in the sixteenth century, and in the seventeenth century 'doh' replaced 'ut' (possibly taken from the Latin word *dominus*, lord). 'Ut' is still to be seen in French music.

Sometimes these names are referred to as the 'Aretinian Syllables'.

dollar

The German for 'valley' is *Tal* – it is from an earlier form of this that we get the word 'dale'. Back in the late Middle Ages there were silver-mines in a place called Joachimstal ('Joachim's Dale'), in Bohemia. The coins which were made there, out of this silver, were called *Joachimstaler*. This was shortened to *Taler*, which became *daler* in Low German and Dutch, and 'dollar' in English.

The curious device $, which is the sign of the American dollar, is a reminder of the pirates of the Caribbean and their 'pieces of eight'. The sign is not derived from the 'S' but is possibly a kind of '8'. The dollar was in origin the Spanish 'piece of eight', which consisted of eight 'reals'. Alternatively the sign may represent the figure of two globes flanked by two pillars, which appeared on the Spanish dollar.

Dollars were first coined in the United States of America in 1794, as a deliberate turning-away from the English coinage. Nowadays dollars are the standard currency in Canada, Australia, New Zealand, Mexico, and many other countries around the world.

dominoes

The game was first known in Europe only about two hundred years ago; it came to this country with French prisoners at the end of the eighteenth century.

A 'domino' was at one time a hooded cloak worn by priests in winter - the word is thought to come from Latin *dominus*, lord. The masquerade outfit worn by Venetians, a hooded cloak with mask, was also called a 'domino'. Many people see the link that would explain the name of the game in the similar appearance of the mask with its eyeholes, and the domino playing-piece with its spots.

donkey

Strange to say, the word 'donkey' was regarded as a slang word until well into the nineteenth century. It probably comes from the word 'dun', which means 'grey-brown'; the 'key' part is a diminutive, so just means 'little'. So a 'donkey' is a 'little grey-brown beast'.

The older more traditional word for a donkey is of course 'ass', an ancient word that appears in Old English as *assa*, comes from Latin *asinus*, and is linked with Greek *onos*. *Asellus*, a diminutive form of the Latin *asinus*, became German *Esel*. (See **easel**)

dotage

To be 'in one's dotage' is to be senile. It comes from an old Dutch word, *doten*, to be silly. Similarly, if you 'dote' on something it means that you have become quite foolish in your liking or love of it.

To be 'dotty', of course, also means to be a bit silly, but it arrives at the meaning by a slightly different route: it comes from 'to dodder' or to be unsteady, and then, by implication, it is linked with senility and stupidity.

drat!

This mild swear-word was once a good deal stronger.

You would hardly guess that it comes from the phrase 'God rot!' This became 'Od rot!' but 'rot' was affectedly pronounced 'rat', so we get, finally, 'drat!'

draughts

As chess was called 'the game of kings', so the game of draughts was, in French, given the name *le jeu des dames*, 'the game of ladies'. In Scotland it is sometimes still called 'dams'.

The name 'draughts' comes from the verb 'draw' and means 'moves'.

duck

Out for a duck! But why 'duck'?

Just as the 'love' in tennis is thought to come from *l'oeuf*, 'the egg', so 'duck' in cricket apparently comes from 'duck's egg', which conveys the same idea: 'O', the shape of 'nothing'!

duffle coat

The town of Duffel, near Antwerp in Belgium, originally made the thick coarse woollen cloth from which 'duffle' coats are sewn.

dunce

John Duns Scotus was a highly sophisticated thinker of medieval times: he became known as the 'Subtle Doctor'. He died in 1308, but his influence on philosophy and theology lasted for two hundred years. His followers were called Dunsmen or Dunses.

But in the sixteenth century, when different ideas were being introduced into Europe, these Dunses opposed the new learning. They were then ridiculed and the word 'Dunce' became a term of abuse.

easel

Blackboard and easel. Blackboard is easy enough to understand; but what about 'easel'?

Just as a donkey patiently bears its load, so does the easel – this is how its name arises. It comes from *Ezel* (the equivalent of German *Esel*), which is the Dutch word for an ass or donkey. One could compare with this word the term 'clothes-horse'.

Easter

Despite the Christian significance of this festival, the name itself comes, according to Bede, from the pagan goddess Eastre, the Anglo-Saxon goddess of the dawn, who was specially honoured at the spring equinox at a great festival called *Eastron*.

It was the policy of the early church to assimilate the features of the old religions but give them new meanings. So, when Christianity arrived with its festival of resurrection, called *Pascha* in Latin, the old Anglo-Saxon name was kept and the feast given a new significance.

A number of Christian festivals and customs have their roots in primitive earlier beliefs, rather as many churches and cathedrals are built on the site of heathen temples.

eiderdown

Properly speaking, eiderdowns should be made from the down of the eider duck, a type of sea-bird found in Northern Europe. The down for 'eiderdowns' is collected from its nest.

A purist might say that a nylon eiderdown is an ornithological insult as well as a linguistic absurdity.

electricity

The first electricity to be encountered was the static electricity got from rubbing a piece of amber. The Greek word for 'amber' is *elektron*, so the word 'electricity', coined in the seventeenth century, means 'the force that is in amber'.

emu

Oddly enough, the large Australian bird which we know as the emu does not get its name from any aborigine word or even English word.

'Emu' derives from the Portuguese word *ema*, which simply means an ostrich.

enthusiasm

God is in the middle of this word – literally!

The Greek word for god is *theos* and this is the word that forms the second syllable of 'enthusiasm'.

If you are 'enthusiastic' you are possessed by a *theos*, or spirit of godlike energy.

equip

This word came through French *équiper* from the Old Norse verb *skipa*, 'to set in order', or 'to man a ship', from *skip*, Old Norse for 'ship'. Since 'equip' has so nautical an origin, it might be maintained that 'equipment' is, strictly speaking, 'boating paraphernalia'.

examination

The Latin word *examen* is thought to have meant the 'indicator' or 'needle' of a balance, and it came to be used for the actual act of weighing, and hence the act of judging. From it came *examinare*, to weigh or consider carefully, and *examinatio*, from which we get 'examination'.

But the French for 'examination' is still the original Latin word – *examen*.

excruciating

This word, meaning 'extremely agonising', comes from Latin *excruciare*, to torture or torment, and has Christian connections in that the centre part of it comes from the Latin *crux*, a cross. The cross was a common method of torture and execution for criminals in the ancient world.

Falkland Islands

The islands were first seen by the British in 1592. But the first settlers were the French, in 1764. These Frenchmen came from Brittany, and called the island *Les Malouines* after their home town, the Breton port of St. Malo. The Argentine name for the Falkland Islands, *Las Malvinas*, is a variation on *Les Malouines*.

The name 'Falkland Sound' was given to the channel between East and West Falkland by John Strong who made the first landing in 1690 – he was honouring the current treasurer of the Navy, Viscount Falkland. Eventually the name passed to the islands themselves.

fan

'Football fans': pop-star 'fans': 'fan' clubs. Where does 'fan' come from?

The immediate answer, of course, is that it is an abbreviation of 'fanatic'. However, fanatic itself has a curious history.

The Latin word *fanaticus* really comes from another Latin word, *fanum*, meaning a 'temple', or 'sacred place'. Those who were devoted to the 'temples' were supposed to be filled with wild religious enthusiasm and were, in effect, *fanatics*!

February

The Latin word *februare* means 'to purify': the name of the month comes from religious rites of purification which the Romans practised during this month. The Roman Catholic Church celebrates the Purification of the Virgin Mary on 2 February.

January and February were added to the previous ten-month year of earlier Roman times (see *January*) and Julius Caesar, to make the calendar fit the solar year accurately, ordered an extra day to be inserted into February every four years between the 23rd and 24th of the month. Tradition maintains that under Caesar's system, February normally had 29 days with 30 every leap year.

Augustus Caesar, when he re-named the month of Sextilis after himself and called it 'Augustus', greedily stole a day from February so that his own month should have 31, and so be equal in its number of days to his great-uncle's month, July.

WITCHCRAFT IN THE CALENDAR

February 2, celebrated by the Roman Catholic Church as the Purification of the Virgin Mary, is one of the four ancient festivals of the Celtic world. As the church became dominant, these older feast-days dwindled away into folklore, celebrated by witches, who remembered the 'old religion'.

February 2 is 'Candlemas', a day still associated with many ancient superstitions. The other three festivals were Walpurgis Night, held on the eve of May Day; Lammas, held on 1 August; and best-remembered of all is Hallowe'en, on 31 October.

Lammas and Candlemas are still kept as Quarter Days in Scotland.

ferret

This animal, a type of polecat used, in hunting, to unearth rabbits, was evidently thought of as 'stealing' its prey. It gets its name ultimately from Latin *fur*, thief. A 'ferret' is 'a little thief'.

fiasco

This is Italian for 'bottle' – English 'flask' comes from it.

A 'fiasco' was originally a failure in musical or dramatic performance and is said to have come from the Venetian glassworkers' slang phrase *far fiasco*, to 'make a bottle' (glassworking being a traditional Venetian art).

Perhaps the point is that when the glass blowers want to make something special and it goes wrong, it gets turned into just an ordinary bottle after all – a fiasco, in fact!

Fiat®

You might suppose that there was a Mr. Fiat, just as there was a Mr. Ford, or a Mr. Rolls and a Mr. Royce. But 'Fiat' is one of those words made up from initial letters: it stands for *Fabbrica Italiana Automobile Torino*, the Italian Car Factory in Turin.

flair

If you have a 'flair' for something you are held to have a special talent or instinct for it. *Flair* is French for 'sense of smell' and comes from the verb *flairer*, to smell; in other words, you have a sensitive 'nose' for whatever it is that is called for.

'Flair' is linked, through the notion of 'smell', with a word that you would probably never associate with it: 'fragrant'! Both come from Latin *fragrare*, to smell sweet.

flower, flour

Although these two words now have quite separate spellings and meanings, they were formerly one and the same word.

One of the meanings of 'flower' is 'the best part' of something: when corn is ground, the finest part is the 'flour'. The spellings began to be differentiated only in the eighteenth century.

flu

Of course this is short for 'influenza' but what may not be generally known is that *influenza* is simply the Italian for 'influence'. The 'epidemic' meaning of *influenza* is however recorded in Italy as early as 1504; it was an infection that raged through Italy and the rest of Europe in 1743 that spread the word to this country.

But why 'influence'? Well, the word comes from the time when people did not know about bacteria and viruses and believed when they were ill that they were under the 'influence' of the stars and planets.

fool

The word 'fool' literally means 'wind-bag'! It comes from the Latin *follis*, which meant a leather bag of any of various sorts – it could be a money-bag, or a pair of bellows, or even an inflated ball – an early version of the football.

forget-me-not

A German legend tells of how this flower got its name from a knight who was trying to pick some of these flowers for his lady-love by the side of a river. He slipped in and drowned, and his last words to her were "Forget me not!" (The German word for this flower is *Vergissmeinnicht*.)

Incidentally, its botanical name is the same as that given to it by the Greeks: *myosotis*, 'mouse-ear'. If you look at the shape of its leaves, you will see how it got the name.

free-lance

When was the last time British soldiers used lances? As late, in fact, as the 1914-18 war. The weapon was not abolished until 1927. A popular medieval weapon for combat between mounted men-at-arms, it had become obsolete with the introduction of firearms, but was revived again much later for use in cavalry charges, particularly by Napoleon.

The word 'free-lance' seems to have come into use in the nineteenth century as a literary term for a member of one of the 'free companies' of medieval times. These were bands of discharged soldiers who offered themselves as mercenaries for any casual war or plundering exploit.

The term 'free-lance' took on: it was used to mean a politician or political writer of no particular allegiance, but now of course is used, chiefly adjectivally, of someone working for himself and not for an employer. Taken literally, 'free-lance' sounds oddly inappropriate in designations such as 'free-lance journalist', or even 'free-lance oboe-player'!

Friday

This day was named after the Anglo-Saxon goddess of love, Frig, in imitation of the Romans who called this day *Veneris dies* after *their* goddess of love – Venus. The Latin name became *vendredi* in French.

Why should superstitious people believe Friday the thirteenth to be an unlucky day? Because it was on a Friday that Jesus was crucified, and, on the night before, at the last supper, after which he was betrayed, the twelve apostles sat down with Jesus, making thirteen in all.

Although Friday the thirteenth has nothing to do with the original 'Egyptian Days', this unlucky or 'dismal' day of modern times does at least help us to understand the superstitious horror that once surrounded these Egyptian dates. (See *dismal*)

Frisbee®

The popular sport of frisbee-throwing has its origins with the Frisbie Pie Company, started about 1871 at Bridgeport, Connecticut. William Russell Frisbie travelled around selling the pies and his sister Susan did the baking.

There is some difference of opinion over whether the proto-type of the plastic frisbee was the Frisbie pie-tin or the Frisbie cookie-tin; however, it is the Yale students who discovered the fun of throwing these baking tins whom Frisbie has to thank for the immortality of his name.

funny bone

This term is rather a weak pun. The anatomical name for the single bone of the upper arm is 'humerus'. (The Romans used the word chiefly to mean 'shoulder'.) If you bang the tip of it at the elbow where the ulnar nerve is exposed, you may not yourself find the resultant agony 'funny', but unsympathetic onlookers might.

galaxy

That beautiful luminous band of stars which stretches right across the heavens is poetically called the 'Milky Way'.

'Galaxy' is in fact the Greek equivalent, for *galactos* in Greek means milk. The Latin and French words for milk, respectively *lac* and *lait*, are also derived from this Greek original. (See **lettuce**)

galvanise

Luigi Galvani (1737-1798), an Italian scientist, made the macabre discovery that he could make a dead frog's legs move when he subjected them to electric shocks. He used two metals to produce the shocks: in the presence of static or atmospheric electricity, he would put one metal in contact with a nerve and the other with a muscle. He attributed the resultant twitching to 'animal electricity' – but what he had, in fact, produced was an electric current. Several electrical processes and devices bear his name in a derived form, but we think particularly of being 'galvanised' or stimulated into activity, like the frog's legs.

gamut

This has come to mean the 'whole range' or 'entire compass' of a set of things. In the past it was, more precisely, the 'whole range' of a set of musical notes.

The term 'gamut' is a curious word-formation that takes us back to the medieval system of musical scales known as 'hexachords'. These were different from our modern musical scales in that they contained only six notes, and they began only on the notes which we call G, C and F. The bottom note of the lowest hexachord was what has become bottom G of our modern bass stave and it was called by the Greek letter *gamma*. Now, in those days, the first note of a scale was known not as 'doh', but as 'ut' (see **doh, ray, etc**.). The bottom note, therefore, came to be known as 'gamma-ut', or 'gamut' for short and so 'gamut' became an easy way of referring to the 'whole range' of hexachords.

geranium

Just as the Greeks saw a dolphin in the nectary of the delphinium, so they saw a crane's bill in the seed-vessel of the geranium. The Greek for a 'crane' is *geranos*.

The name 'cranesbill' is given to several wild species of geranium.

Gestapo

Everyone knows about the secret state police in Hitler's Germany, but it's not often people wonder how they got that sinister-sounding name.

Actually, it's formed by the first letters of the German words for secret state police: *Ge*heime (secret) *Sta*ats *po*lizei (state police).

gherkin

Gherkins, of course, are small cucumbers used for pickling.

The odd name goes back a long way, and has its word-ancestry in many languages, ultimately deriving from the Greek word *agouros*, which meant 'unripe', or 'youth'. Perhaps it was because gherkins look a bit like unripe cucumbers.

gin

'Gin' is an abbreviation of 'geneva', the older name of this drink, which is itself really the Dutch word *genever* remodelled to match the place-name, Geneva. *Genever* was formed from the Old French *genevre* (now *genièvre*), juniper, from Latin *juniperus*. Traditionally, gin was a spirit distilled from grain or malt, flavoured with juniper berries.

gladiolus

This flower is linguistically linked, through Latin *gladius*, sword, with the combatants in the ancient Roman arena: a 'gladiator' was so called because he was armed with a sword; the 'gladiolus' meaning 'a little sword', got its name from its sword-shaped leaves.

gnome

It was a rumbustious sixteenth century eccentric, Theophrastus Bombastus von Hohenheim, who called himself Paracelsus, who invented the word.

He wrote 364 works, on a huge variety of topics, mainly medicine. Swiss by birth, he never settled anywhere for long because of his aggressive love of argument. Eventually he was murdered in Salzburg in 1561.

His word 'gnomus' refers to sprites guarding the interior of the earth and its treasures, and probably derives from the two Greek words *ge-nomos*, meaning 'earth-dweller'.

Little did he think that four and a half centuries after his death there would be plastic gnomes on sale as garden decorations.

FAIR PIXILATED!

Just think of the wealth of words we have for fairies – most of them coming from ancient folklore: elves, pixies, brownies, dwarves, trolls, goblins, hobgoblins, imps, sprites, leprechauns, flibbertigibbets, sylphs, cluricaunes, pigwidgins, bogies . . .

And J.R.R. Tolkien has given us the Hobbit! *(See **nickel**)*

golliwog

The creator of the 'golliwog' character was a New York author of children's books, Florence Upton. She wrote *Adventures of Two Dutch Dolls and a Golliwogg* (two 'g's!) in 1895. Perhaps she did not actually invent the word, but it was in 1895, thanks to that book, that it firmly entered the English language.

The character in Florence's book was based on rag dolls, popular in America at that time.

Florence Upton is buried in Hampstead Cemetery, London, with a golliwog on her tombstone!

The final syllable, 'wog', is so sensitive these days that the famous golliwog on pots of jam has now had to be renamed to become just 'Golly'.

'Golliwog' may well have prompted this offensive bit of slang. But 'wog' has also been explained as '*w*ily *o*riental *g*entleman'.

Another suggestion is that it comes from the letters stencilled on the back of clothes worn by navvies constructing the Suez Canal between 1854 and 1869. The letters stood for 'Workers on Government Service', thus proving that they were genuine employees, and not just hangers-on.

goodbye

This is a prayer compressed into one word. It is a short version of 'God be with you'.

gorilla

Amazingly, this word existed for more than two thousand years before the gorilla itself was discovered, in the 1840s.

The story of the word goes back to the fifth or sixth century BC, when a Carthaginian explorer called Hanno sailed along the coast of Africa. He discovered a tribe of 'hairy women' and, according to the Greek account of the event, called them *gorillai*.

The word was therefore known for thousands of years before a suitable creature was found for it.

gosh!

The word 'God', used as a swear-word, is clearly a blasphemous offence to many people, so there have been a number of artificial variations. 'Gosh!' is one of these.

Similarly, there is 'Golly!'; 'Good Gracious!'; 'Good Grief!'; and, with a change of vowel from 'o' to 'a' (see also *drat*), 'Gad!'; 'By Gad!'; 'Begad!'; 'Egad!', etc.

The same tendency to steer away from actually mentioning God is found in other languages, such as French, in which they change '*par dieu!*' into '*parbleu!*'

gossip

'Sib' is an Old English word for 'related' or 'relation'. 'Godsibs' were sponsors for a child at baptism – or perhaps it would be better to call them 'God-parents'.

The word came to be applied to female friends and acquaintances, especially those invited to be present at a birth, who no doubt stood about chatting and became, in fact, 'gossips'!

graffiti

The word 'graffiti' did not come into use until the nineteenth century, and then it was deliberately invented to describe the wall-scratchings in ancient cities such as Pompeii and Rome.

During archaeological digs at Pompeii these scratch-marks were found to be very important, giving an idea of what daily life was really like in those days.

But marks have always appeared on walls and buildings. In the eighteenth century 'Alexander the Corrector' (his name was Alexander Cruden, the author of the famous Biblical concordance) used to carry a damp sponge about with him everywhere he went, to rub out the graffiti which offended him.

greengage

Sir William Gage, a botanist, of Hengrave Hall, Suffolk, introduced a green plum into England from France, about the year 1725. Its colour and his name became permanently associated in the name given to this succulent fruit – the 'green gage'.

grenade

We are familiar with the grenade as an efficient military weapon. The name is French and, curiously, means in origin 'pomegranate'. The small hand-bomb gets its name because it looks like the fruit.

From 'grenade' comes the 'grenadier', the soldier who threw grenades. In French, *grenadier* is both the grenade-throwing soldier, and a pomegranate tree.

greyhound

The 'grey' in 'greyhound' has nothing to do with its colour. It comes from Old Norse *grey*, a bitch, so that the 'greyhound' really means 'bitch-dog'.

grocer

At one time this meant a wholesaler, or a trader who dealt *en gros* – in bulk. The small tradesman was then called a 'spicer', or spice-seller, which is our equivalent of the modern French *épicier*.

grog, groggy

'Grogram' was a coarse-grained cloth, getting its name from the French *gros grain*, or 'coarse thread'.

The eighteenth-century British admiral, Edward Vernon, became known as 'Old Grog' because of the coat he wore, made of this material.

In 1740, when Commander-in-Chief West Indies, he ordered watered-down rum to be served to both officers and men. Naturally, this made him very unpopular and the mixture itself was nicknamed 'grog'.

So, if you take too much 'grog', or more generally nowadays if you are feeling unsteady or unwell, you say you are feeling 'groggy'.

groundsel

This common little weed has the most extraordinary origin to its name. It was used in ancient times in poultices, and because it helped to cure sore places in the flesh, it became called the *gundeswilge* which is Old English for 'pus-swallower'. Repulsive, but true!

guillotine

It can't be good for one's historical image to have an instrument of death named after oneself, but this is what happened to the Frenchman, Dr. Joseph Guillotin. In fact, he did not invent the guillotine, but he strongly advocated its use, during the time of the French Revolution, because he thought it the most humane way of killing people!

The machine was at first called *La Louisette* but became known as *la guillotine*. From that time on, capital offenders in France were 'guillotined' rather than hanged.

gymnasium

A 'gymnasium', literally, is 'a place of nudity', from the Greek word *gymnos*, nude.

In ancient Greece, the *gymnasion* was the place where youths wrestled naked, exercised, and received training for competition. Gymnasia were provided by the state, and, as an important feature of city-life, began to be places not only of physical education but of intellectual instruction too (see **academy**).

It is not so surprising after all, therefore, that in Germany a *Gymnasium* is a grammar-school.

gypsy

People used to think that the gypsies came from Egypt; their name is derived from 'Egyptian'. In fact, they come from India, as their language, Romany, proves.

They came to Europe in the fifteenth century, and were a mystery people. The French thought they came from Bohemia, and called them 'Bohemians'.

hallowe'en

'Hallowe'en or 'All Hallows' Eve' is the name given to 31 October, the day before All Saints' Day. The word 'hallow' means 'a holy one' or 'saint'.

But before Christianity came to Britain, 31 October was kept as a Celtic festival called 'Samhain' marking the end of the summer; it was also the eve of the new year. The festival was primarily an agricultural one, but was also associated with the dead, whose souls were believed to visit their former homes at this time. Thus the legends of ghosts who roam the air this night come from a set of beliefs more ancient than ours – it was traditionally a time when the dead wandered forth.

Hallowe'en is one of the four ancient festivals celebrated before the coming of Christianity. *See Witchcraft in the Calendar*, next to the entry on *February*. Also, *see May.*

hammock

Christopher Columbus noticed that the natives of the West Indies often used to sleep in nets, and the word 'hammock' itself passed from the Carib language first into the Spanish as *hamaca*, and then into English as 'hammock'.

hamster

If you have ever kept hamsters you will know that they stuff their nests and cheek-pouches with uneaten food. The name is German (from an earlier Germanic word meaning 'corn-weevil') and this habit of the animal has given rise to the German words *hamstern*, to hoard, and *Hamsterer*, a hoarder.

The golden hamster comes from the Balkans and the Middle East; those used in laboratories are all descendants of a hamster family captured in Aleppo, Syria, in 1930.

handkerchief

The word 'kerchief' really means a 'head-covering', from the two French words, *couvre*, cover, and *chef*, head.

When people began to carry a smaller piece of cloth for (among other purposes) blowing their noses into, the name 'hand-kerchief' was given to it, a refined word that concealed its somewhat crude function.

A more realistic-sounding term for it, in former times, was a 'muckender' or 'muckinger' from a provincial French version of *mouchoir*, handkerchief.

harrowing

Most town-dwellers do not really know what a harrow is, although they may use expressions such as 'a harrowing experience'. A harrow is a heavy, metal, spiked grid, which you drag across the land to break up the soil. Its tearing action is responsible for the meaning that 'harrowing' has, of rending or lacerating the feelings. *(See **hearse and rehearsal**)*

---

haversack

'Sack' is understandable, but why 'haver'?

It's simple really. We find *Hafer* in German, and 'haver' in English dialect, meaning 'oats'. A 'haversack' was the bag in which people used to carry food for their horses – an oats-bag.

---

haywire

Bundling up bales of hay requires very tightly stretched wire, and sometimes this wire can snap, resulting in a disastrous mess of scattered hay and entangled wire.

It is no doubt an image of total confusion of this sort that is conjured up by the expression 'all haywire'. In fact the adjective 'haywire' (which comes from the US) was originally used to mean 'ill-equipped' or 'inefficient', from the practice of making hasty repairs to equipment with 'haywire'.

hazard

There are two possible derivations for this word. The more likely is through Spanish *azar*, chance, from Arabic *al zar*, 'the die'.

A more picturesque derivation comes from William of Tyre, a twelfth-century historian, who says that during the Crusades a castle in Syria at a place called Hasart was under siege, and the 'hazard', the game of chance played with dice, was invented during that siege.

hearse

Today we use the word 'hearse' for the vehicle in which a coffin is transported. In years gone by, however, a hearse was the actual coffin or bier. This was how Shakespeare used the word, for instance in *Julius Caesar* (III, 2, 169): "Stand from the hearse; stand from the body".

Before that, 'hearse' was the name used for a sort of framework for candles, put around the coffin at a funeral. This framework got its name because it looked rather like a harrow – for the word 'hearse', especially in its earlier spelling 'herse', originally meant 'harrow'.

'Herse' could also mean 'portcullis', the sharp pointed ends being reminiscent of a harrow's spikes. Incidentally *herse* is still the French word for both 'harrow' and 'portcullis'. *(See **harrowing and rehearsal**)*

By heart

Why is it 'by heart'? When you learn something, so as to be able to reproduce it word for word, why don't you learn it 'by liver', for example, or 'by kidneys'?

An attractive explanation is that 'by heart' is a translation of French *par coeur*, but that the expression had originally been *par choeur*. *Choeur*, pronounced the same as *coeur*, means 'choir'.

When you learn by chanting, in a group, as young children learn their multiplication tables, you are learning *par choeur*, 'in a choir', not *par coeur*, 'by heart'!

helicopter

Literally, a helicopter is a 'screw-wing', from the Greek words *helikos* and *pteron*. *Helikos* gives us the word 'helical'. The 'pter' part is also found in the name of that hideous old monster, the pterodactyl, which means 'wing-fingered'.

hippopotamus

Like the rhinoceros, this animal was known in antiquity and its name, which comes from ancient Greek, means 'river-horse', from *hippos*, horse, and *potamos*, river.

HISSING THE MYSTERY LECTURES!

The Reverend Dr. William Archibald Spooner was a Doctor of Divinity and Warden of New College Oxford, a kind man and a great scholar whose astonishing claim to fame is that he seemed to suffer from a kind of verbal dyslexia. In fact he was an albino and suffered from very poor eyesight.

A 'spoonerism' is the name of a phrase in which the initial letters somehow get transposed, so that a 'half-formed wish' becomes a 'half-warmed fish'.

Once he told one of his students that he had 'hissed all my mystery lectures and tasted two whole worms' (missed all my history lectures and wasted two whole terms!). He ordered the student to leave Oxford by the 'town drain'.

Other "spoonerisms" include:

'The Lord is a shoving leopard'   'Kinkering Kongs their titles take'

'riding on a well-boiled icicle'   'a cat popping on its drawers'

And Queen Victoria is said to have been startled to be addressed as 'my Queer Dean'!

---

hoax

This word is believed to have come from the 'hocus' part of 'hocus-pocus'. But what is the origin of 'hocus-pocus'?

'Hocus-pocus' was used both as a name for a conjuror, and by conjurors as a magic formula. In all probability it is a contraction of a sham Latin phrase of the sort used by quack doctors.

But there is an ingenious if far-fetched seventeenth-century suggestion. The words "This is my body" were spoken by Jesus at the Last Supper, and they are used at the solemn moment of consecrating the bread in the Communion Service. The Latin words were *Hoc est corpus*; it was conjectured that 'hocus-pocus' was an ignorant version of this, used as a kind of 'transformation' formula in imitation of the Latin words by which the bread was transformed into Christ's flesh.

---

hogmanay

This strange name used, especially in Scotland and Northern England, for the last day of the year, has its roots in ancient folklore and is of very uncertain history.

It is fairly certain, at least, that it is of French origin. In this country, and on the continent, it was the tradition for children, on 31 December, to call at houses asking for cakes and gifts. The word 'hogmanay' was used not only for the day, but also for the gift; this matches exactly the use of the northern French dialect word *hoguinané*, and its original Old French form *aguillanneuf*. In Guernsey the form is *hoginono*, in Spain *aguinaldo*.

The second part of *aguillanneuf* is easily seen as *l'an neuf*, the new year. It was once suggested that the whole word represented *au gui l'an neuf*, 'to the mistletoe the new year'; even that 'hogmanay' might be corrupted form of *au gui menez*, 'lead on to the mistletoe'. Mistletoe was thought to have been used in the ceremonies of the Druids of ancient Gaul and Britain.

Robert Chambers in his *Book of Days* mentions the speculation based on the children's rhyme which used to be sung at the doors of neighbours to ask for the Hogmanay cakes:

"Hogmanay, Trollolay,

Give us of your white bread, and none of your gray."

Another favourite rhyme was:

> *Get up, Goodwife, and shake your feathers,*
> *And dinna think that we are beggars;*
> *For we are bairns come out to play,*
> *Get up and gie's our hogmanay!'*

. . . adding, rather gruesomely,

> *Get up, Goodwife, and binna sweir* (slow),
> *And deal your bread to them that's here;*
> *For the time will come when ye'll be dead,*
> *And then ye'll neither need ale nor bread.'*

Perhaps the children's favourite, however, was:

> *My feet's cold, my shoon's thin;* (shoes)
> *Gie's my cakes, and let me rin!'* (run)

It has been put forward the 'Hogmanay, Trollolay' are corrupted forms of *Homme est né, Trois Rois là* – 'A man is born, three kings are there' – a reference to Christ's nativity.

holiday

A 'holiday' as is generally known, was originally a 'holy day' or religious festival. People might be released from their work on such days, and the meaning 'a day on which normal work is suspended' was established by the sixteenth century (and hence the 'period' of recreation or festivity). It was, however, up to your employer: it was with great reluctance that Scrooge in Dickens' *Christmas Carol* allowed Bob Cratchit to have Christmas Day off.

With the introduction of official Bank Holidays in 1871, which were kept also by business organisations, the British worker began to establish his right to leisure. Many of the holidays, of course, fell on the old 'holy days'.

hooligan

There is a widely believed tradition that the original Hooligans were an Irish family who lived in the Southwark district of London in the late nineteenth century. Their surname was really Houlihan, and their way of life was so notoriously lawless that their name, slightly altered, became a byword for trouble-making.

horse chestnut

Horse chestnut trees are relative new-comers to Europe, coming from Constantinople (now Istanbul) in the sixteenth century. The first horse chestnut in England came in 1600.

By why **horse** chestnut?

Well, the report that came from Turkey at that time was that the conkers were fed to sick horses. Normally, of course, animals will not eat them, but according to Gerard in his *Herball* of 1597, '. . . people of the East countries do with the fruit thereof cure their horses of the cough.' (See *conkers* and *chestnut*)

humble pie

The expression 'to eat humble pie' is perhaps not so frequently heard nowadays as formerly. It was used of someone forced to acknowledge that he was in the wrong, and confess to a fault, such as failing to do something on time.

But 'humble' in this expression has nothing to do with humility – 'umbles' were the poorest part of a stag: to 'eat humble pie' is to eat a pie of venison giblets.

A GAGGLE OF GIGGLES
A CURIOUS COLLECTION OF COLLECTIVES

A 'collective noun' is a name given to a group of creatures. The English language is astonishingly rich in these terms. Here are just some of them:

an army of caterpillars
a bale of turtles
a barren of mules
a bevy of roe-bucks
a bouquet of pheasants
a brood of hens
a building of rooks
a business of ferrets
a cast of hawks
a cete of badgers
a charm of finches
a clowder of cats
a colony of ants
a colony of penguins
a company of parrots
a congregation of plovers
a cover of coots
a covey of partridges
a cowardice of curs
a crash of rhinoceroses
a deceit of lapwings
a descent of woodpeckers
a dissimulation of birds
a dray of squirrels
a drift of hogs
a drove of cattle
a dule of doves
an exaltation of larks
a fall of woodcocks
a flight of swallows
a flock of sheep
a gam of whales
a herd of elephants
a gaggle of geese (on water)
a gang of elk
a harras of horses
a host of angels
a host of sparrows
a hover of trout
a husk of hares
a kindle of kittens
a knot of toads

a labour of moles
a leap of leopards
a litter of pups
a murder of crows
a murmuration of starlings
a mustering of storks
a nest of rabbits
an ostentation of peacocks
a pace of asses
a paddling of ducks
a parliament of owls
a party of jays
a peep of chickens
a pitying of turtle-doves
a plague of locusts
a pod of seals
a pride of lions
a rafter of turkeys
a rag of colts
a richness of martens
a route of wolves
a school of fish
a school of porpoises
a shoal of bass
a shrewdness of apes
a siege of herons
a sloth of bears
a skein of geese (in flight)
a skulk of foxes
a smack of jellyfish
a sord of mallards
a sounder of swine
a spring of teal
a string of ponies
a swarm of bees
a tiding of magpies
a trip of goats
a troop of kangaroos
an unkindness of ravens
a walk of snipe
a watch of nightingales
a wedge of swans

Why a 'Dule' of Doves?

The strange word 'dule' comes from the French *deuil*, mourning, Just listen to the mournful sound that doves make!

humour

It was thought in the Middle Ages that your character came from a mixture of four kinds of fluid in your body. These fluids were called 'humours', from the Latin word, *humor*, moisture. ('Humid' and 'humidity' are related to it.)

The four 'humours' were bile (choler), black bile (melancholy), blood and phlegm, and the proportions in which they were mixed in your body determined your personality. 'Humour' took on the meaning 'disposition', giving us words like 'good-humoured' and ill-humoured'. It could also mean a passing mood, an inclination or caprice – hence a whimsical, fantastic or comical turn of mind, leading to the modern meaning, 'wit'.

imp

This word has an intriguing history. It is possibly connected remotely with Greek *emphutos*, implanted, and medieval Latin *impotus*, a graft. Its earliest meanings in English are 'young shoot' and 'graft'.

It came to mean 'offspring' or 'child', and, used in such expressions as 'imp of Satan' and 'the Devil's imp', it took on the meaning 'little demon', and finally the 'mischievous little so-and-so' that is now implied by the word.

infantry

It may seem strange, but until quite recently (1969, in fact) anyone aged under 21 was legally known as an 'infant'.

Latin *infans* meant literally 'non-speaker', in other words, a baby; but in Late Latin the word has the meaning 'young man'. Italian *infante*, 'youth', acquired the additional meaning 'foot-soldier'. From it came *infanteria*, foot-soldiery, which became English 'infantry'.

The 'infantry', therefore, were originally 'the young men', who normally fought on foot, whereas the older, richer men were mounted on horseback.

inoculation

Oculus is Latin for 'eye', so an 'oculist' is someone who deals with your eyes.

But *oculus* can also mean 'bud', and it is this sense that is used in the word 'inoculation'. You 'inoculate' a plant by inserting a bud (from another plant that you wish to propagate) under its bark.

So 'inoculation' is the 'implantation of an organism' into your body.

insect

The obvious feature about an insect is that it is *in sect*ions – and this is how it gets its name.

The Latin word *secare* means 'to cut'. So an 'insect' is something that seems to be 'cut' or divided up into little bits.

intoxicated

'Intoxicated' means 'drunk'. But the 'tox' part means 'poison'. If you are 'intoxicated' you are 'poisoned' with alcohol.

The source is archery. *Toxon* was the Greek word for a 'bow'. *Toxicon pharmakon* was 'poison used in archery', poison smeared, in fact, on the arrow-tip. This arrow-poison became *toxicon* for short, and gives us the words 'toxic', 'toxicology', 'toxicity', and many more.

ironmonger

The 'monger' part of this is worth attention. We use it in a few compound words, such as 'fishmonger', 'scandalmonger', 'ironmonger', but it is an odd word inasmuch as we cannot use it universally: we cannot talk of a 'bookmonger' or a 'shoemonger', nor can we use 'monger' as a separate word, as we can, for instance, use 'broker'.

In fact, 'monger' comes from the Latin word, *mango*, a term for a somewhat disreputable trader or dealer. It originally meant 'slave-dealer'.

Islam

'Christianity', obviously enough, is a religion based on the teachings of Christ. But what about 'Islam'? The word is Arabic, and its meaning is 'surrender' – surrender, of course, to God.

jackdaw

In the middle ages this bird was simply a 'dawe' – but as everyone called him 'Jack' daw, so he came to be known universally as a 'jackdaw'.

The same has happened to a number of birds and animals. Exactly the same name was given to 'Jack ass'.

For similar names, see ***robin, magpie, wren***.

January

In the earliest Roman calendar, there were ten months, with a two-month gap in the winter. The year began in March. When under Numa Pompilius, the second king of Rome (who died in 672 BC), or possibly under the later Etruscan dynasty, the months of Januarius and Februarius were introduced to replace the gap, the year was still thought of as starting in March and it wasn't until 153 BC that it officially began in January.

It was appropriate that it should do so, for Januarius was the month dedicated to Janus, the god of doors and beginnings, who had two faces, one looking forward and one backward. His name is to be seen in Latin *janua*, a door, and in English 'janitor', a 'door-keeper'.

jeans

'Jean' was the name of a strong cotton material that came originally from the city of Genoa, whose French name is Gênes.

Round about 1860 an American sail-maker started making his jean sailcloth into trousers. His name was Levi Strauss: hence, 'levis'.

jeep

During World War II jeeps were to be found everywhere: the perfect general-purpose car.

And this is what they were originally called – 'General Purposes Vehicle', or G.P. for short. Somehow the very name 'jeep' was just right for them.

Jerusalem artichoke

Brussels sprouts came from Belgium, but Jerusalem artichokes certainly never came from Palestine! In their case, the name 'Jerusalem' is really a highly imaginative version of *girasole*, the Italian name for 'sunflower'.

Literally, the *girasole* is a 'turn-sun', so named in reference to the way in which these flowers always turn to face the sun.

The 'Jerusalem' artichoke is a species of sunflower, with edible tuberous roots. The only connection it has with the other, 'globe', artichoke, is that they are supposed to taste alike.

not a jot

Well, what *is* a 'jot'?

It's simply the Greek letter *iota* – the equivalent of our 'i', and the smallest letter in the alphabet.

We use 'iota' too, to mean the smallest bit: – 'There's not an iota of truth in what he said!'

journey

Nowadays we can travel non-stop as far as we please, probably suffering 'jet-lag' in the process. Our ancestors were apparently much more sensible: a 'journey' was just as far as one could properly travel in a 'day' (from French *jour*, day). In medieval times this was about twenty miles.

jubilee

The 'jubil' part of this word is the Hebrew word *yobel*, a ram. The 'Jubilee' was a special year among the Jews, every fifty years, in which people were forgiven their debts, Israelite slaves were emancipated, and goods and property returned to their original owners or their heirs. To mark this special time a blast was blown on a ram's horn.

Strictly speaking, then, a jubilee should occur every fifty years, but 'silver jubilee' has been introduced to mean a 25th anniversary; and Queen Victoria celebrated a 'Diamond Jubilee' of sixty years.

For the origin of the celebration of a 'jubilee year' see the book of Leviticus in the Bible, Chapter 25, verses 8-17.

juggernaut

We hear all too often about 'juggernaut' lorries speeding along our roads and through our towns and villages. Where does the expression come from?

In Hindu mythology 'Jagannath' was a form of the god Vishnu, and it was in this form that he was worshipped at the town of Puri. A huge idol of Jagannath was dragged through the streets every year on a gigantic cart, and devoted worshippers of the god were said, in the exaggerated reports of European witnesses, to throw themselves under this and get themselves squashed to death.

The name comes from Sanskrit *Jagannatha*, 'Master of the World', from two words, *jagat*, world, and *nathas*, lord.

juke box

The word 'juke' is something of a curiosity. It is West African, and crossed to America with the captured black slaves.

Originally it meant 'disorderly' or 'noisy'.

A HARMLESS DRUDGE

Dr. Samuel Johnson single-handedly produced his great Dictionary in 1755. A person who compiles a dictionary is known as a 'lexicographer' (after the Greek *lexis*, a word). Johnson himself was known in his lifetime as 'The Great Lexicographer'.

However, with dry humour, in his own dictionary he defined a 'lexicographer' as simply 'a harmless drudge'.

Today, we use the word 'dyslexia' to refer to someone who is having difficulty with words.

July

The first person to make the calendar fit neatly into the solar year was Julius Caesar. His system, according to tradition at least, ran like this, with 31-day months alternating with 30-day months: Januarius, 31 days, Februarius, 30 (in leap years only); Martius, 31; Aprilis, 30, Maius, 31; Junius, 30; Quintilis, 31; Sextilis, 30, September, 31; October, 30; November, 31; December 30.

After Julius Caesar was assassinated, Mark Antony changed the month of Quintilis to 'July' in honour of Julius who was born in this month.

Then, when Augustus Caesar renamed the month of Sextilis after himself, he gave it 31 days, and this confused the rest of the calendar. He had to readjust the days in September, October, November and December.

jumbo

The most famous elephant of all time, Jumbo, was an African elephant who lived in London Zoo a hundred years ago. He was eventually sold to an American circus in 1882 and was killed by a train in 1885. His stuffed body is still on view in Boston, USA.

His name has become not only a sort of nickname for any elephant, but also a designation means 'extra-big' or 'outsize', used, for instance, on cornflake packets, but most notably applied to massive transatlantic aircraft.

June

The origin of the name of this month was disputed even in Roman times, some claiming that its name, *Junius*, honoured the goddess Juno, and some that the month had originally been dedicated to the *juniores*, the young men, as opposed to the elders or ancestors, *majores* (who, according to this theory, were remembered in the name *Maius*. May). Others again have connected it with the Roman *gens* (family) of Junius.

junk mail

'Junk' was at one time a sea-farers' term for old, discarded cordage. Then it became used as their slang word for tough bits of salted meat – probably looking a bit like chunks of old rope. Then, after a while, it extended its meaning to any unwanted rubbish.

As for 'mail', the word goes back even further. It comes directly from an old French word, *male*, meaning a bag. In fact a 'mail-bag' is something of an absurdity: a 'bag-bag'.

junket

This curious word comes from the Latin word, *juncus*, a rush – the sort of rush you make rush-baskets and rush-mats with. At one time fresh cream and cheese were brought to market laid in or on reeds or rushes.

A cream cheese was prepared in a 'junket' or rush-basket, and took on the name of the container. The name also passed to the familiar dish made with curds and cream.

Later, the word came to mean a delicacy or dainty dish, and then a feast or banquet, giving us 'junketing', a roistering celebration – a far cry from the original humble rush-basket.

kaiser

The German word *Kaiser* comes originally from Caesar, the family name of the first Roman emperors. It was used as a general term for an 'emperor', but is more famous as a title: it was the title of the Holy Roman Emperor, of the Emperor of Austria (from 1804), and of the Emperor of Germany (from 1871).

kangaroo

There is a popular story that when the famous explorer and discoverer of Australia, Captain James Cook, first saw this animal, he turned to a native and asked him what it was. The native, who did not know what Cook was saying, replied "Kangaroo" – which meant, in his aborigine language "I don't understand!" Hence the name.

However, 'kangaroo' was a genuine native word for the animal, from *kanga*, a verb meaning 'to leap'.

kite

Wildlife, alas, is becoming so rare that few people have seen the real living bird, the kite, as it hovers over its prey.

The toy kite simply gets its name from the bird, but now that the bird is so scarce, we hardly remember that once the word was a symbol of speed and ferocity.

knave

'Knaves' are 'yobs' – by definition, you might say, but in fact pretty well literally, too.

A 'knave' was originally just a 'boy', the equivalent of German *Knabe*, but the word took on the meaning 'an unprincipled rogue'. 'Yob', a nineteenth-century slang backspelling meaning no more than 'boy', came to mean 'lout'.

But why *should* these words develop such derogatory meanings? Presumably because knaves *are* yobs – or, in other words, boys will be boys!

knots

Knots! why should ships measure their speed in 'knots'?

The explanation can be found in the old practice of reeling out a line over the stern which had a number of knots tied at regular intervals. The sailors would then measure the speed of the ship by counting the number of knots run out in a given time.

KNOTS IN MAY?

The old rhyme 'Here we go gathering nuts in May' is a corrupted form of 'knots of may'.

In this context, a 'knot' is a posy and 'may' refers to the flower and not the month. No 'nuts' are ripe for gathering in

---

lady

This word is of ancient origin as you might expect. It comes from Old English *hlaefdige*, which meant, literally, 'bread-kneader'. *Hlaf*, meaning 'bread', is the word from which 'loaf' is derived.

---

ladybird

This little creature presents us with a bit of a puzzle.

The 'lady' in 'ladybird' is the Virgin Mary, the mother of Jesus. A 'ladybird', therefore, is 'Our Lady's bird'. And this seems to be no isolated piece of religious folklore with regard to this insect. In French it is called *bête a bon Dieu* or 'the good God's animal'; in German it is a *Marienkäfer* or 'Mary's beetle'; in Dutch it is a *lieveheersbeestje* or 'the dear Lord's beast'; in Spanish it is a *mariquita* or 'little Mary', also *vaca de San Antón* or 'cow of Saint Anthony'; in Russian it is *Bozhya korovka* or 'God's little cow'. In Danish it is a *mariehøne*, or 'Mary's chicken'.

Why, in such a diversity of countries and languages, should the ladybird have this link with religion?

lark

Our slang word 'lark' about is derived from an earlier word *laik*, to play, which came from the Saxon *lac*, a contest. And perhaps this in turn is linked with the name of the bird, with its effortless ability to soar into the air 'skylarking' about.

The poetic collective noun for these birds is a perfect description: an 'exaltation' of larks. (See ***toad***)

larva

'Larvae' are ugly-looking creatures, not quite alive and not quite dead, often deathly-white in colour.

It does not come as much of surprise to realise that 'larva' is the Latin word for a 'ghost' or 'spectre' or perhaps a 'mask'. (See ***bug***)

laser beam

Most people are familiar with the term 'laser beam', but it takes a physicist to remember that 'laser' is an acronym for *l*ight *a*mplification by *s*timulated *e*mission of *r*adiation.

lavatory

The odd thing about a 'lavatory' is that it is merely a 'place where you wash yourself'. In the cloisters of Gloucester cathedral you can see a *lavatorium* (the word from which 'lavatory' comes) which was genuinely the monks' 'wash-place'. *Lavatorium* comes from the Latin *lavare*, to wash (from which French *laver*, to wash, comes). Even a 'latrine' was originally a *lavatrina*, from the same word.

'Privy', 'water-closet', 'toilet', 'powder-room', 'loo', and now the imaginative American 'comfort-station': euphemism has succeeded euphemism and evasion evasion in the attempt to avoid indicating the real function of the place. The trouble with such euphemisms is that they don't stay euphemisms for long, so the process of renaming the 'little room' looks like continuing.

leek

The word 'leek' anciently used to mean simply 'plant', and so it appears, somewhat disguised, in other names too: 'charlock', 'garlic' and 'hemlock' are all varieties of 'leek'.

It is the national emblem of Wales, and the story goes that St. David ordered his Welsh compatriots fighting under the leadership of King Cadwaladr to wear a leek in their hats, so as to distinguish them from their Saxon adversaries.

The fictional Fluellen in Shakespeare's *Henry V* talks of it as 'an honourable padge (badge) of the service'.

lens

A lens is shaped rather like a lentil (a kind of bean), and gets its name from this vegetable – *lens* is the Latin word for 'lentil'; and in French, *lentille* means both 'lentil' and 'lens'.

> ### lent
>
> The name Lent is not, in its derivation, at all religious. It comes from the Anglo-Saxon for spring, *lencten*, which is related to 'length' and refers to the lengthening of the days at this time of the year. In Dutch *lente* still means spring, and *lentemaand* is a name for March.

leopard

It was once believed that leopards were not a separate species at all, but the result of crossing a lion with a panther. This Greek name for a lion was *leon*, and for a male panther was *pardos* (giving us the archaic English 'pard'); so the imaginary cross-breed was called, in Greek, a *leo-pardos* or 'lion-panther'.

leotard

Jules Léotard, a French trapeze artist born in 1830, shares with Lord Cardigan the distinction of having a common article of clothing named after himself. Dancers and gymnasts owe a debt to Jules Léotard. He died in 1870.

The French, by the way, call a leotard a *justaucorps* – formerly a 'jerkin'.

lettuce

When you next cut a lettuce, notice the white juice coming from the stalk. It is this 'milk' that gives the lettuce its name.

Just as Latin *lac*, milk, became *lait* in French, so Latin *lactuca*, lettuce, or the 'milky plant', became *laitue* in French. It is from *laitues*, plural of *laitue*, that we get 'lettuce'.

lilac

This beautiful name means, literally, 'blue', or rather, 'bluish', from the Persian word *nilak*.

The first plants of the common lilac came into the country from Eastern Europe via France about the year 1600, but the garden lilac, with intensely purple flowers, was introduced direct from Persia in 1640.

lino

– Or, more formally, 'linoleum': but how did a late-nineteenth-century invention get so Latin-sounding a name?

This is a good example of the practice of quarrying the ancient languages for suitable words to make into names for newly-discovered substances and phenomena. 'Linoleum' in fact is the original manufacturer's made-up word, put together from two Latin words: *linum* flax (from which we get 'linen'); and *oleum*, oil. Lino is composed of canvas coated with oxidised linseed oil.

lieutenant

The name of this officer is French, and means 'holding a place': *lieu* is French for 'place'; and *tenant* means 'holding'. So, what he is doing is simply holding a place' in the rank of officers.

It is worth noting that 'lieutenant' is pronounced differently according to whether the officer in question is in the army or in the navy: (which one is 'leftenant' and which one is 'lootenant'? (see bottom of page)

loo

What a lot of strange words and expressions we use for lavatories!

Gents, ladies, toilets, lavs, geographies, little rooms, powder rooms, smallest rooms, WCs, latrines, ablutions. Old folk can remember privies, earth closets, heads and even thunderboxes. And before that there were bogs and jakes and the old monks had their reredorters.

There must be hundreds of words and euphemisms. The Americans add to the list with their term 'Comfort Station'.

The word 'loo' is something of a puzzle. Mostly it has been explained by supposing that it is derived from 'gardyloo' – an English form of the French for 'Mind the water', shouted by people emptying their chamber-pots out of bedroom windows.

But it could come from a sort of pun on 'Waterloo' – referring to water closets. Or perhaps it comes from French hoteliers who used to put 00 or 100 on toilet doors – and this became misinterpreted as 'loo'.

The army officer is 'left' and the naval officer is 'loot' or 'le'.

lord

Since the word 'lady' means 'bread-kneader', it is perhaps not surprising to find that 'lord' is also connected with bread.

It comes from two Old English words, *hlaf*, bread, and *weard* (which became 'ward'), guardian. So, a *hlafweard* was a 'loaf-ward' or 'one who guards the bread'.

love-thirty, love-forty

Why 'love' in tennis?

No-one is certain, but some people, on the grounds that tennis is in origin a French game, derive the word from *l'oeuf*, 'the egg'. An egg is shaped like an 'O' – that is, 'nought', or the score of 'nothing'. *(See **duck**)*

lunatic

Why is a lunatic called after the moon? The belief that there is a connection between the moon and madness is an ancient one. The word comes from Latin *lunaticus*, moon-crazed, from *luna*, moon. At one time the law made a distinction between those who were 'insane' or permanently and incurably mad, and those who were 'lunatic' or only now and then moved to madness by the moon.

There are serious scientific reports that demonstrate that arson, kleptomania, dangerous driving and homicidal drunkenness all show noticeable increases when the moon is full – and that this holds good whether the night is moonlit or cloudy. So there may be some support for the age-old theory that connects fits of madness with the phases of the moon.

LOONY OR JUST PLAIN MOONSTRUCK?

Have you ever thought what a lot of euphemisms and slang words there are for being mentally deranged or perhaps just a bit eccentric? There must be scores of English words.

'Loony' and 'moonstruck' obviously derive from the effect of the moon. But here is a collection of words which have unknown or obscure origins, all meaning 'barmy': (incidentally, 'barm' is the froth on fermenting liquor)

bonkers	crackers	scatty	screwy	wacky
nutty	batty	cuckoo	cranky	potty
daft	dippy	dotty	bananas	loopy

and of course there are phrases galore, such as:

a screw loose   bats in the belfry   a tile loose   not all there
off one's rocker   up the creek   round the bend   soft in the head
Many of these are passing slang, but there are always more words to replace those that are lost.

How many more phrases can you add to the list?

---

lychgate

A lychgate is one of those covered gates at the entrance to a churchyard. They are found most usually in country churchyards and are considered rather picturesque. People even make gates of a similar kind for their front gardens, and call their homes 'Lych Cottage' or something like that.

The appearance may be attractive; the word is a bit gruesome! It comes from German *Leiche*, corpse; the covered gates were originally used for giving shelter to a corpse on its way to a burial. So, a lychgate is really a 'corpse-gate'!

We find this word for 'corpse' again in 'lyke-wake', an all-night watch kept over a dead body.

macabre

The 'Danse Macabre' or 'Dance of Death' was a famous and popular series of pictures, sometimes accompanied by verses, that were copied in murals, stained glass and printed books throughout Europe in the late Middle Ages and showed Death, as a skeleton, visiting victim after victim and leading them to their fate. Popes, emperors, kings, merchants, doctors, ploughmen, children: all were led away by the gleeful, gloating, dancing skeleton.

The word 'macabre' certainly comes from the phrase 'Danse Macabre', but there is much debate as to how 'macabre' should be explained etymologically. There have been theories that Macabré was the name of the artist who first depicted the Dance of Death, in a Paris church in 1424; that it was the name of the author of the verses accompanying the pictures; that the word 'macabre' is connected with Hebrew *meqaber*, gravedigger; that, rather, it refers to the seven martyred brothers in *Maccabees* in the Apocrypha.

macintosh

Charles Macintosh's surname is a household word, frequently shortened to the simple 'mac' that we take with us in wet weather.

Born in 1766 in Glasgow, he became a chemist and in 1823 he patented his invention, a material composed of two layers of fabric bonded together with an adhesive formed from coal naphtha and india-rubber – a substance that rendered the material waterproof.

This ingenious chemist, like many inventors, bequeathed his name to the article he created – his waterproof material. The name passed easily to the indispensable garment made from it. But Macintosh can be credited with a second achievement: by virtue of his Highland name, beginning with 'Mac' (meaning 'son of'), he bestowed an entirely new meaning on that ancient Gaelic prefix.

The Real McCoy

The Real McCoy was an American boxer, whose original name was Norman Selby, born in Indiana in 1873.

He changed his name to 'Kid McCoy' because it sounded Irish, and the boxing world at that time always expected great things of Irish boxers.

He won the world welter-weight championship in 1896 and continued to enjoy great success and fame. And when another boxer came along, whose name was Al McCoy, the 'Kid' billed himself as the *Real McCoy*.

This isn't the end of the story, however, because the phrase 'the real Mackay' had already been used, originating in Scotland in the 1880s to refer to whisky of superb excellence.

The expression seems to have had a kind of double origination.

madeira

From Madeira, the Atlantic island, we get the name of a sherry-like wine that is made there as well as that of a rich sort of cake. But the word 'madeira' has a curious background.

The Romans used the word *materia* to mean 'wood'. It could also mean, more vaguely, 'stuff', and we have developed the rather general terms 'material' and 'matter' from it.

The Portuguese, however, turned the word *materia* into *madeira*, and in Portuguese it still means 'wood'. When Portuguese sailors discovered this island in the Atlantic they thought it so well-'wooded' that they called it 'Madeira' – the 'wood-island'.

magnolia

Magnolia gets its name from Pierre Magnol (1638-1715), professor of botany at Montpellier. The outlandish look of some plant-names is often to be explained by their being Latinised forms of a surname, usually that of a naturalist or botanist. Here are some other examples from the long and international list of eponymous flowers:

Aubrietia, from Claude Aubriet, 1665-1742, a French naturalist and painter; Begonia, from Michel Bégon, 1638-1710, a French promoter of botany; Buddleia from Adam Buddle, who died in 1715, an English botanist; Camellia from Josef Kamel, a Moravian Jesuit who collected plants in the Philippines; Clarkia from Captain Clark, who died in 1838, an American explorer; Dahlia from Anders Dahl, who died in 1789, a Swedish botanist; Forsythia from William Forsyth, 1737-1804, a British botanist; Freesia from F. H. T. Freese, a German physician who died in 1876, or H. Th. Frees, another German physician, or E. M. Fries, a Swedish botanist; Fuchsia from Leonard Fuchs, 1501-1566, a German botanist; Gardenia from Alexander Garden, 1730-1791, an American botanist; Gloxinia from B. P. Gloxin, a German botanist of the eighteenth century; Lobelia from Matthias de Lobel, 1538-1616, a Flemish botanist; Poinsettia from Joel Poinsett, 1779-1851, American Minister to Mexico; Wistaria from Caspar Wistar, 1761-1818, An American anatomist. (See also **tradescantia**)

magpie

The first name, 'Margaret' has many shortened forms: Mag, Madge, Maggie, Margot, – and, in earlier days, Maggot.

The magpie's original name was simply a 'pie' – which it earned by being so 'pied' in colour: black and white.

As happened with so many creatures, our ancestors gave it a first name as well: Margaret, or rather 'Maggot'. And 'Maggot Pie' has been shortened nowadays to just 'magpie'.

In *Macbeth* Shakespeare talks of 'magot-pies, choughs and rooks'. (See also **robin**, **wren** and **jackdaw**)

manoeuvre, manure

By derivation both these words mean 'to work by hand'. Latin had a phrase *manu operare*, to work by hand, from which came two Old French verbs: *manuevrer*, which became 'manoeuvre', and *manouvrer*, to 'till the soil', which became 'manure'.

The verb 'manure' has had a variety of meanings, among them 'to occupy', to administer', 'to till or cultivate'; but the noun 'manure' that comes from it has always been a rather politely evasive name for dung or compost.

March

The Romans honoured Mars, the god of war, both in their name for Tuesday, *Martis dies*, and in the name *Martius*, the month of March. Originally, March began their year; even in England, from 1400 until 1752, the legal year began on 25 March. In French the connection with the god looks even closer than in English for the French for March is *mars*.

margarine

The name of this butter-substitute has a lofty Greek source. It is derived from *margaron*, a 'pearl'. One of the fatty constituents of margarine was called 'margaric acid' because of its pearly appearance; the name 'margarine' comes from it.

marmalade

There is a wealth of fanciful suggestions for the origin of this word. The true derivation is this: it comes from Portuguese *marmelo*, meaning 'quince'. But this is not the end of the story, because *marmelo* itself is derived from Greek *melimelon*, which is made up of two words, *meli*, honey, and *melon*, apple. The *melimelon* was apparently a sweet apple grafted on a quince.

So, the Greek 'honey-apple', or rather, the Portuguese quince, made into a preserve, gave us the word 'marmalade'.

An odd fact is that in the other European languages that use the word, 'marmalade' is a general term for 'jam'; only in English is it used exclusively of the kind of preserve made from citrus fruits.

martin

House martins get their name from the Christian name Martin. They may have been given this name because they appear in March (the *Martian* month) and then they disappear about the time of St. Martin's Day, (11 November).

masochism

Those who wish to know more about this aberration should read the novels of the Austrian writer Leopold von Sacher-Masoch (1836-1895), from whose name the word is derived. 'Masochism', about which he writes, is the seeking of what would normally cause pain to oneself, in order to gain sexual pleasure. The term is now more generally applied to a liking for being dominated or cruelly treated.

mausoleum

When King Mausolos of Caria died in 353 BC, his widow, Queen Artemisia, ordered a magnificent tomb to be erected at Halicarnassos in his memory. Huge, and splendidly decorated with statues and friezes by leading sculptors of the day, the Mausoleum was one of the ancient Seven Wonders of the World. Sculptures from the sepulchre are still to be seen in the British Museum. Nothing remains above ground at the actual site.

Words last longer than buildings, however. This erstwhile wonder of the world may now be almost forgotten, but Mausolos remains enshrined more permanently in the word 'mausoleum'.

May

Even the Romans could not decide whether the name of this month, *Maius* (from which comes English 'May' and French *mai*), was derived from the name of the goddess Maia or was called after the *majores* (perhaps meaning 'elders' or 'ancestors'), or really meant the 'month of growth and increase' through a possible connection with *magnus*, big.

May was considered an unlucky month for marriages even by the Romans. May Day, with its maypole, May Queen, superstitions, and tradition of witchcraft, has connections both with the pre-Christian Celtic festival of Beltane, marking the beginning of summer, and with the Roman flower-festival held at this time, the Floralia.

may-bug

The name is self-evident: this large, rather clumsy bug flies about in May and June. It is also called a cockchafer.

A curious country name for it is 'Bishop Barnabee', and there is an old rhyme:

Bishop, Bishop Barnabee,
Tell me when my wedding shall be;
If it be tomorrow day,
Ope your wings and fly away.

Does anyone know the origin of this? (See *cockchafer*)

mayday ... mayday ...

When people are in distress, this is the signal that is sent out, asking for help. But why 'mayday'? Why don't they shout out 'hallowe'en' or even 'Boxing Day'?

The fact is that mayday has nothing to do with the 1st of May – it is simply the French *m'aidez* – which means 'help me!'

melancholy

The literal meaning of this word is 'black bile', from two Greek words, *melas*, black, and *chole*, bile.

The significance of 'black bile' is to be found in the medieval belief that there were four liquids or 'humours' inside you. If you have a predominance of black bile you were inclined to be sullen, sad and depressed – suffering, in fact, from 'melancholy'. (See *humour*)

microbe

This word caused quite a fuss when it was invented, by a Dr. Sédillot, in 1878. French language-experts complained that the Greek words *mikros*, little, and *bios*, life, strictly added up to a word meaning 'short-lived' rather than 'a small creature'.

However, the word was handy as a name for disease-causing organisms and was used widely before the words 'bacteria' and 'virus' came to be preferred.

midwife

'Wife' here has its older meaning, 'woman' – but why 'mid'?

It is the equivalent of the German word *mit*, meaning 'with'. A 'mid'wife is a woman who is 'with' the mother at childbirth, to assist her.

migraine

If you suffer from migraine you will know how acutely painful this type of headache can be. Sometimes the pain can be very closely restricted to one part of your head, and this feature is the origin of its name.

It comes from the two middle syllables of Greek *hemikrania* or 'half-skull' (from *hemi*, half, and *kranion*, skull), meaning 'pain in one side of the head or face'.

mob

A good 'English' word – but originally it was an abbreviation of the Latin word *mobile* in the phrase *mobile vulgus*, meaning the 'fickle multitude' or 'excitable rabble'. In the Latin, *mobile* means 'easily moved' or 'excitable', and it is *vulgus* that means 'crowd' or 'rabble'.

But it was *mobile* rather than *vulgus* that was extracted from the phrase during the seventeenth century to mean 'the crowd' and finally shortened to 'mob'.

mole

The name of this little burrowing animal has been used a great deal simply to mean a 'spy' or someone who is working in secret, and so 'mole' is gradually extending its meaning. But why is a mole called a mole?

Centuries ago this little creature was given a much longer and odd-looking name: 'mouldwarp'. In fact, there were many variations: mowdiewarp, moudiewart, moudiwort, etc. And in Germany it was called a *Multwurf*, and in Dutch, a *Muldvarp*.

The point about all these variations is that they all meant 'earth-thrower'! The first part of the name was simply 'mould' or 'earth', and the second part was an old word *weorpan,* 'to throw'. So a mouldwarp was simply a creature that threw earth about. It's a pity that no-one calls them mouldwarps nowadays – but if you're lucky you can still find very old countrymen who use it as a part of their country dialects.

Monday

English 'Monday', German *Montag*, Dutch *maandag*, Danish *mandag*, etc., all mean 'Moon-day'. They are translations of the Latin *lunae dies*, 'day of the moon', a variant of which, *lunis dies*, turned into *lunedi* in Italian, and *lundi* in French. Even in Greek the day was called *hemera Selenes*, day of the moon.

It was the day that was evidently traditionally associated with the worship of the moon throughout pre-Christian Europe.

money

A most curious history attaches to this word. The Latin verb *monere* means 'to warn' and one of the titles given to the goddess Juno was *Juno Moneta* or 'Juno the Warner'.

A part of Juno Moneta's temple in ancient Rome was set aside for making coins, and the word *Moneta* gives us not only 'money' but also the 'mint' where it is made.

monk

The first 'monks' were hermits who lived alone. They did not live in monasteries with other monks, but lived alone, perhaps in caves, or in the deserts.

The Greek word *monachos*, meaning 'alone', gives the essential meaning of a 'monk'.

monster

It was formerly believed that strange events and misshapen animals were warnings from God.

The word comes from the Latin *monstrum*, whose original meaning was 'an evil omen' (from *monere*, to warn). So a 'monster' can be thought of as a 'warning-creature'.

morris dance

Why 'Morris'?

The word is an altered form of 'Moorish'. Morris-dancing is said to have had a Moorish or Arabic origin; an alternative suggestion by Cecil Sharp, the collector of folk-songs and folk-dances, was that the dancers used to blacken their faces to disguise themselves and so looked like 'Moors'.

mumbo-jumbo

An expressive word for meaningless rubbish!

The original Mumbo Jumbo was a deity worshipped by the Mandingo tribes of West Sudan in the form of a grotesque idol. The African form of the word is thought to have been *Mama-dyambo*. It is through the idea of this idol as an object of unthinking veneration or awe that the present meaning, 'impressive-sounding nonsense', has developed. At least Mumbo Jumbo has the consolation that he has a permanent shrine in the English language

mummy

The bandaged, embalmed corpse known as a 'mummy' gets its name from one of the substances believed to have been used in the process of mummification. Arabic *mumiya*, a mummy, originally meant 'bitumen' – a substance that the Egyptians were thought to cover the corpses with. *Mumiya* comes from Persian *mum*, wax, so you could facetiously argue that a 'mummy' is a 'waxwork'.

MUM!!   MUM!!!

In nearly every language the word of 'mother' begins with the letter 'm'.

It has been suggested that the easiest sound a child can make, simply by opening its mouth, is the 'm' sound, so inevitably 'mum-mum-mum' is taken to mean the person closest to it – its mum. In fact, there's only one other sound to be made by merely opening your mouth – and that is pa-pa!

In the English-speaking world mothers are often call mum, mummy, ma, mamma, mam, mom. Here are a few 'mummy-words' in other languages:

mater (Latin)	mère (French)	Mutter (German)	madre (Spanish)
me (Vietnamese)	mu (Chinese)	mat' (Russian)	mitir (Greek)
mam (Welsh)	mor (Norwegian)	man (Hindi)	umame (Zulu)

---

muscle

The origin of this word does not readily occur to you, though you don't have to go far to find it. It comes straight from the Latin word for 'muscle' – *musculus*, meaning literally 'a little mouse'!

The shape of a muscle, resembling a mouse with a trailing tail, gives it is name.

narcissus

The Greek legend tells of a handsome young man, Narcissus, who fell in love with his own reflection in a fountain. He pined away and was changed into the flower we now call by his name.

The story gives us also the word 'narcissistic' – a term we apply to people who are inclined to admire themselves rather too much.

nasturtium

This is one of those flowers whose names, on analysis, prove full of interest. 'Nasturtium' is believed to mean, literally, 'nose-twister' – a name the plant got because of its pungent smell.

The word is derived from Latin *nasus*, nose, and *torquere*, to twist.

naughty

The word 'naughty' is really only used nowadays of children, but was at one time a much stronger term of censure, used of people quite criminally wicked. "Thou naughty varlet!" says the constable Dogberry to his prisoner Conrade, in Shakespeare's *Much Ado about Nothing* (IV, 2, 77).

It originally meant 'needy, having nothing', and then 'inferior, worth nothing'; it comes from the word 'naught', meaning 'nothing'.

In the Authorised Bible, Jeremiah speaks of 'naughty figs, which could not be eaten' (Jeremiah xxiv, 2), but later translators have changed 'naughty' simply to 'bad'.

nave

The nave of a church is the main body, where the congregation sits. But why is it called a 'nave'?

Because of its resemblance to a ship. Look up into the vaulted roof of a great parish church and you will see that it looks like the inverted hull of a wooden ship.

The word comes from Latin *navis*, ship, from which come, French *nef*, nave, as well. In Spanish *nave* means both 'ship' and 'nave'. German *Schiff* and Dutch *schip* have both meanings, too. Latin *navis*, of course, also gives us 'navy'.

navvy

Why is a man who digs with pick and shovel called a 'navvy'?

An older word for a 'canal' is a 'navigation' and in the eighteenth century, when the canals and waterways were being dug, the workmen who dug them were called 'navigators' – or 'navvies' for short.

nazi

An ugly word, but it is simply two syllables from the German political party of the National Socialists, i.e. *Na*tional*so*zialist.

Properly pronounced ('Natsee') it sounds, perhaps, brisk and efficient: but during the war Winston Churchill invariably used to make it sound sinister and sluggish, as he snarled out 'Narzy'!

neighbour

This comes from Old English *neahgebur*, made up of the ancestors of the two words, 'nigh' and 'boor'. A 'nigh boor' was a 'nearby dweller' or 'nearby farmer'. The word 'boor' developed to mean a 'peasant', hence someone who has 'rustic' behaviour or is clumsy, rude and ill-mannered.

The Dutch word for 'peasant' or 'farmer' is *boer*. This is how the Dutch farmers who settled in South Africa came to be known as 'Boers'.

nest egg

People often use the term 'nest-egg' but seldom realise exactly what it actually used to mean. The original 'nest-egg' was a pottery egg which was put into a hen's nest to encourage it to lay other eggs around it.

A financial 'nest-egg' is capital which helps us to add more to it with the extra interest.

nephew

Our word 'nephew' actually comes from the Latin word for a grandson – nepos. From this Latin original we also derive our word 'nepotism', meaning the corrupt practice of giving jobs and perks to members of one's own family.

nice

'Nice', universal term of approval that it is, is one of the more overworked words in the language. 'Nice day!', 'a nice cuppa tea'; 'Nice to see you!' Yet the word from which 'nice' is derived, the Latin *nescius*, 'ignorant' or 'stupid', is startlingly distant from it in meaning. 'Nice' came into English from Old French; the French *nice* is defined by Randle Cotgrave in his French-English dictionary of 1611 as 'lither, lazie, sloathfull, idle; faint, slacke; dull, simple'.

Quite how the meaning has changed through the centuries it would be impossible to show in detail here. In Chaucer's time, 'nice' still meant 'foolish', but could also mean 'wanton' or 'lascivious'.

By the sixteenth century, it had acquired the meanings 'tender', 'delicate', 'coy'. 'fastidious', 'particular' and 'precise'. But in 1818, in *Northanger Abbey* (Chapter XIV), Jane Austen's hero Henry Tilney was able to scoff at the current usage in his day, very like our own: ". . . this is a very nice day, and we are taking a very nice walk, and you are two very nice young ladies. Oh, it is a very nice word indeed! – it does for everything . . . now every commendation on every subject is comprised in that one word".

nickel

German miners who were looking for copper were often disappointed and deceived by nickel ore, which looked like copper ore but yielded no copper. They called it *Kupfernickel* or 'copper-devil'.

It was a Swedish mineralogist, Axel von Cronstedt, who first shortened this mining nickname to 'nickel' after he had succeeded in obtaining the metal from its ore in 1751.

The story of the word 'cobalt' is very similar. German miners looking for silver ore would frequently come across another ore that they thought not only worthless, but also destructive to the silver ore, and they called it *Kobold*, 'imp' or 'goblin'.

nickname

Apart from its use as a verb in the phrase 'to eke out', the word 'eke' has been lost from the language. It used to be an adverb meaning 'also', and a noun meaning an 'addition' or 'piece added on'.

A 'nickname' is in origin an *eke*name, or an 'extra name'. The 'n' of 'an' became transferred to 'eke' to make it 'neke', which became 'nick'. For a word which lost its initial 'n' in a process the reverse of this, see *umpire.*

nightmare

The 'mare' part of this is an Old English word for a kind of female night-monster or incubus which was believed to come and sit on your chest while you slept, and produce bad dreams.

The French for 'nightmare' is *cauchemar* – containing the same word. *Cauchemar* literally means 'the monster who tramples on you'!

noon

When King David wrote "Seven times a day do I praise thee because of thy righteous judgements" (Psalm 119, v. 164), he little knew what his words would lead to.

Taking him literally, the Catholic Church instituted seven church services in each day. St. Benedict, in his famous Rule, wrote that "This sacred number seven will thus be fulfilled by us if, at lauds, at the first, third, sixth, ninth hours, at vesper time and at *completorium* we perform the duties of our service". As Chaucer remarked, this Rule was "somewhat strict"!

The service of Nones, whose name comes from Latin *nona*, the ninth hour (by the Romans reckoned as the third hour before sunset) was held at 3.00 pm, but could , in later time, be held earlier. 'Noon' which also comes from *nona*, and was associated with the time of the Nones service, crept backwards similarly through the day, till, by the thirteenth century, it meant 'midday'.

Nosey Parker

George Orwell once wrote that 'The most hateful of all names in an English ear is Nosey Parker'. And it's perfectly true that we don't like other people prying into our private lives.

Tradition has it that the original 'Nosey Parker' was Matthew Parker, Archbishop of Canterbury under Queen Elizabeth I. He was a great scholar and did much to establish the Church of England, producing the Bishop's Bible in 1572. Perhaps by enforcing conformity to his revised services he gained his unpopularity

nostril

This word is made up of two words: 'nose-thirl', or, 'nose-hole'. We no longer use the word, 'thirl', but we have its variant, 'thrill', which is really 'something which bores into you', and also, closely linked with this, is 'drill', which of course, makes a hole.

November

From Latin *novem*, nine. When the Roman calendar had only ten months, this was the ninth. The Anglo-Saxons used to call this month *Blot-monath*, 'sacrifice-month': it was the month when they made sacrifices and slaughtered cattle so that they could salt down the meat for the winter.

The traditional Dutch name for November is *slachtmaand* or 'slaughter-month'.

oboe

The old form of this word, which you still sometimes see on the organ-stop that produces a sound imitative of the oboe, is *hautboy*, from French *haut bois*, 'high wood'. The hautboy was a treble member of the woodwind family of shawms. The lower instruments of the family were *gros bois*, 'great wood', and the bassoon was one of these.

October

Until the second century BC the Roman year began in March, so October used to be the eighth month of the year. Its name comes from Latin *octo*, eight. For more than two thousand years this name, along with 'September', 'November' and 'December', has been inappropriate and out of date.

odds bodkins!

A quaint old swearing expression. Literally, 'by God's little bodies!' Although it sounds rather silly to us, in fact it was a strong piece of blasphemy. God's 'little bodies' were the pieces of bread used to signify his body in the Catholic Mass. These were regarded as particularly sacred, for they were God's own person. So, to swear 'by God's little bodies' was a serious matter!

ZOUNDS!

There are quite a number of other swear-words connected with various aspects of God. 'Zounds' is an old swear-word much used in the works of historical novelists. It is a contraction of 'by God's wounds!' – which had become ''swounds' or 'zounds'.

People would swear 'by God's death' ('sdeath!'), 'by God's blood' (''sblood!), and even 'by God's nails', meaning the nails that fixed Jesus to the cross (''snails').

O.K.

No-one can say for certain where this expression came from, but there has been no lack of suggestions. The explanation that deserves most support is this: O.K. are the initials of 'orl korrekt', a jocular spelling of 'all correct'. The source of the joke may have been a comment by President Jackson of America on a man whose character was being called in question, that he was 'ole kurrek' and his papers should be marked 'O.K.' In 1839 'O.K.' became well-established, and was used in 1840 as an election slogan for the democratic presidential candidate, Martin Van Buren, which cleverly exploited the initials of his nickname 'Old Kinderhook' (he came from Kinderhook in New York).

A less credible theory is that it comes from one of the languages of the African slaves, brought over to America in slave-ships. On the Guinea coast there is a language called Wolof in which 'yes' is said to be *waw*, and *kay* to mean 'very much'. So, 'yes, certainly' is *waw kay* – turning easily into 'O.K.'

Even more far-fetched is the following. The Latin word *hoc*, this, came to be used in French for 'yes'. After the fall of the Roman empire the French dialect in the north dropped the 'c' and added *il*, giving *o'il* – and this turned into the modern French *oui*.

Meanwhile, in the south of France, they kept closer to the Latin form, with *oc*. The two dialects were in fact named after their forms of the word 'yes' – the *Langue d'oil* in the north, and the *Langue d'oc* in the south.

The story claims that *oc* crossed the channel, and the Atlantic, and became Scottish 'och aye' and American 'O.K.'

Old Nick

This is another name for the Devil. It does not, surprisingly enough, come from the name, Nicholas. It derives from the German word, 'Nick', meaning a spirit or demon. *(See **nickel**)*

There are many picturesque words for the devil: Old Hornie, Old Clootie, Prince of Darkness, and of course Satan (which means 'enemy' in Hebrew). 'Lucifer' was the the brightest of all God's angels: the name literally means 'Bearer of Light', but in legend Lucifer aspired to become greater than God, and was therefore banished to live as 'Satan', ruler of Hell.

onion

'Onion' and 'union' both come from the Latin *unio*, oneness, or unity, from *unus*, one. *Unio* could also mean a single large pearl and became a countryside name for an onion, possibly because both pearl and onion are composed of a series of layers forming a single whole or 'union'.

A 'union' was a 'pearl' in English too. In the duelling scene that ends Shakespeare's *Hamlet*, Claudius promises that "in the cup an union shall he throw", in reference to the pearl that will be the prize.

orchestra

Although nowadays the word 'orchestra' means a group of instrumental players, its first meaning was 'dancing-place'. It was originally the space in front of the main acting area in the ancient Greek theatres, where the chorus danced and sang.

It was not until the seventeenth century, when the first Italian operas were being performed, that the word began to acquire its present meaning, that is, the musicians themselves rather than the place they occupied.

orchid

It may come as something of a shock to realise the 'orchid' is simply the Greek word for 'testicle'.

The point is that the bulbous roots are somewhat testicle-shaped.

Pakistan

The name Pakistan sounds so appropriate for a country of the Indian sub-continent that one would not think of asking its origin. But it is a kind of acronym, first used in 1933. It comes from the initial letters of the old Indian states that form the country: *P*unjab, *A*fghan Frontier, *K*ashmir, *S*ind, and the last part of Baluchi*stan*, making 'Pakstan'. This name *can* apparently be given a local interpretation as the land (*stan*) of the pure (*pak*).

The 'i' crept in later, for ease of pronunciation.

pal

The word 'pal', meaning a friend, is vaguely thought of as being 'slang' and therefore not 'really' a word at all. However, like all slang words, it has an interesting history, and in actual fact it is one of the small number of Romany words to have come into use in our English language. Romany is the language of the Gypsies, and it has its origins in an Indian dialect in north-west India: it is probably thousands of years old.

palace

The Roman Emperors had their luxurious residence on the Palatine Hill, called the Palatium, one of the seven hills on which Rome was built. All 'palaces' can thus be said to take their name from this Roman hill.

pamphlet

It was a popular twelfth-century Latin poem called *Pamphilus seu de Amore*, 'Pamphilus, or About Love' that gave us this word. Presumably, copies of it were distributed in large numbers.

The title was shortened to *Pamphilet* in Old French, and the word came into general use for little booklets of similar type, giving us the Middle English word *pamflet*. 'Pamphilus', literally, means 'beloved of all'.

panic

Pan, the Greek god of herds, flocks and pastures, was believed to induce a sudden supernatural terror in people, causing them to rush in headlong flight, like cattle.

The word 'panic' comes from the Greek adjective *panikos*, formed from the god's name, and was originally thought of an an adjective itself: this groundless terror was known as 'panic fear', or 'panic terror', which became shortened to 'panic'.

The name Pan came from *paon*, a 'pasturer', but even the Greeks confused it with *pan*, 'all'.

pantomime

'Pantomime' comes from the Latin *pantomimus*, a mimic actor, from Greek *pantomimos*, an 'imitator of all'. The *panto-* part means 'all', and *mimos*, a 'mimic'. The Roman *pantomimus* was an actor who performed in dumbshow, by miming, and it was to this kind of actor that the English word 'pantomime' originally referred. But in the eighteenth century a type of ballet was invented, usually based on one of the myths of Greece or Rome, but including the traditional characters of Italian comedy (see *pants, zany*) and these entertainments were called 'pantomimes'.

Finally came the Christmas show, based on a nursery tale, with broad comedy, clowns, and a transformation scene.

pantry

It is not immediately obvious why a pantry should be so called, but the mention of French *pain*, bread, may give a clue. 'Pantry' comes from *paneterie*, a 'bread-closet' in Old French.

'Larder' is now pretty well synonymous with 'pantry', but it used to be the place where you kept your 'lard' (pork-fat or fat bacon).

pants

The word 'pants' has its origin in the Italian theatre. San Pantaleone was a popular saint in Venice, and the name Pantaleone was common amongst Venetians – so much so that in the Italian popular theatre 'Pantaleone', shortened to 'Pantalone', was a stock Venetian character, a doddering old man in long or baggy trousers. He became a 'pantaloon' in English: in Shakespeare's *As You Like It* (II, 7, 158), 'the lean and slipper'd pantaloon' is the sixth and penultimate age of man.

'Pantaloons' became a name for trousers or breeches, of various styles, and this came to be shortened to the form we use today, 'pants'.

Strictly speaking, 'pants' are trousers (as in the US) not the garment underneath.

paraffin

'There's nothing like it!' is the meaning of this name. It is coined from Latin *parum*, little, and *affinis*, similar. The substance was discovered in 1830 by Karl, Baron von Reichenbach, a German scientist and industrialist, and it was its remarkably neutral quality – its lack of affinity for, or reaction to, other substances – that made him christen it 'paraffin'.

pantechnicon

This odd word has an odd history. Literally, it comes from two Greek words and means 'belonging to all the arts.' Originally it was the name of a bazaar selling artistic works, situated in Belgrave Square, London.

However, this bazaar went out of business and the premises turned into a furniture store. The old name, 'Pantechnicon', still continued to be used for the delivery vehicles of the new business. It still means a furniture van.

paraphernalia

Surely a queer-looking word for odds and ends. Its origin is even queerer – it comes from the ancient Greek law on marriage.

A *pherne* was a dowry, or the goods which the husband was given when he married his wife. *Para* means 'beside' – so the things from the bride's family which were 'para pherne' were the articles that were not really part of the dowry, and the married woman could legally claim these as her own. They were called *parapherna* in both Greek and Latin, and *paraphernalia bona* (bona means 'goods') in medieval Latin, and finally just *paraphernalia*. Under English and Scottish law, the whole of a wife's property became her husband's and the term 'paraphernalia' was restricted to her most personal possessions – her clothes and her 'odds and ends'.

patter

The comedian's or conjuror's 'patter' has an oddly religious origin. It comes from Latin *pater noster*, 'Our Father' – the first two words of the Lord's Prayer. When you gabble your prayers, you are literally 'pattering'.

peach melba

The name of Dame Nellie Melba (1861-1931), the Australian opera singer, was so renowned throughout the world that it became the fashion, during her lifetime, to name new commodities, foods, clothes, etc. after her. The French chef Escoffier devised a dish of peaches and ice-cream served with cream and raspberry puree ('Melba sauce'), which he called 'Peach Melba' in her honour.

She was really Helen Armstrong (née Mitchell). It was in 1887 that she took the name Melba from her native town – Melbourne, Australia.

pencil

'Pencil' used to mean a 'paint-brush'; it comes from latin *penicillus*, a paintbrush, or literally 'a little tail'. It was not until the late sixteenth century that an early type of 'dry pencil' was invented – a piece of graphite in a holder, but as it improved and became popular over the centuries, the name 'pencil' gradually came to be used exclusively for this instrument. Interestingly, the German word *Pinsel* means 'paint-brush'.

pen-knife

What have pens got to do with knives?

Pens used to be made from large feathers or 'quills'. People had special little knives with which to cut and fashion the base of the feather into a nib.

The original meaning in English of 'pen' was 'feather': it comes from *penna*, the Latin word for feather. In French, *plume* means both 'feather' and 'pen'.

person

The origin of this common English word takes us back to early Roman times when actors used masks. A *persona* was a stage mask, and it was believed to be so named because an actor had to *speak through* it (from *per*, through, and *sonare*, to make a sound) in order to make himself heard.

Some language historians prefer to trace *persona* back to the word *phersu*, a mask or masked figure, from Etruscan, another early language of Italy. It is thought, in any case, that both *persona* and *phersu* are related to Greek *prosopon*, face, mask, character in a play or story, and hence, person.

Peter

Is your name Peter? If so, you share it, as you are bound to know, with the apostle, Simon. He was nicknamed 'Cephas', the Aramaic word for 'rock', because of his size and strength; the name was translated in the New Testament into the Greek word for 'stone' – *petros*.

Jesus was making a pun (which is reproduced in the Greek version) when he says "Thou art Peter (*Petros*), and upon this rock (*petra*) I will build my church" (Matthew, Chapter 16, verse 18).

petrol

Petrol is manufactured from the mineral oil 'petroleum'. The word 'petrol' is a shortened form of this (originally medieval Latin) word; it means 'rock-oil' – from *petra*, rock, and *oleum*, oil.

philately

Most people know that a 'philatelist' collects stamps, and that 'philately' is stamp-collecting.

The French word *philatélie* was made up in 1864 by a Monsieur Herpin, who put together, in a rather cumbersome fashion, the Greek prefix *phil-*, loving, and the Greek word *ateles*, 'tax-tree' (from *a*, not, and *telos*, tax); so its meaning was 'the loving of that which is untaxed'.

Until the nineteenth century, it was the recipient of a letter who paid for its carriage, not the sender. Sometimes letters would be 'franked' – stamped or marked in some way that showed that they were to be carried free of charge. When methods of reforming the postal system were being considered by Rowland Hill in the 1830s, he proposed that the sender should pay for the carriage, and that a small sticky label should be affixed to the back of the letter to show that such payment had been made. The letter came, in other words, 'free of charge' or 'untaxed' to the recipient.

Philip

If your name is Philip, then you are, or should be, a 'lover of horses'. The 'phil' part is the Greek prefix meaning 'loving' and the 'ip' part comes from Greek *hippos*, horse.

philosopher

The Greek thinker, Pythagoras, who was born about 580 BC, is said to have rejected the title *sophos*, meaning 'wise man'. He thought it too arrogant and asked to be called *philosophos* instead, which meant 'lover of wisdom'. This rather deprecatory title became *philosophe* in French, and 'philosophre', then 'philosopher', in English.

phlegmatic

The connection between phlegm, the unpleasant discharge when we cough, and 'phlegmatic', meaning 'calm' and 'not easily moved to strong feelings', takes us back to the Middle Ages when phlegm was one of the four liquids or 'humours' in the body, the mixture of which gave you your temperament. It was thought that an excess of 'phlegm' produced a cold and sluggish character. (See *humour*)

photography

This is another invention which has been given a Greek-derived name. The reason why Greek is so often used for this purpose is simply that at one time Greek was so universally known that it was a sort of international language of educated people.

Photos means 'light'; and *graphikos* means 'writing', so that 'photography' really signifies 'writing with light'.

piano

Early keyboard instruments such as the harpsichord did not have a great range of softness and loudness. When the 'pianoforte' was invented in the early eighteenth century, the important thing about it was that it could play both loudly and softly. The name is Italian, composed of *piano*, 'soft', and *forte*, 'strong' or 'loud'. The word was being used in its short form 'piano' by the beginning of the nineteenth century.

'Piano' comes from Latin *planus*, level, from which we get, in English, the grassy 'plain' as well as the carpenter's 'plane'.

piggy-bank

If you have a piggy-bank, it is probably shaped like a pig. The name did not come from its shape, but from the material it was made from. 'Pig' or 'pigg' is a Scots and Northumbrian name for an 'earthenware pot', or simply for 'earthenware'.

The 'piggy-bank', or as it was often known, the 'pig', assumed the shape of the animal through the association of the two words. 'Pig' or 'piggy' was a name also given to stoneware hot-water bottles. There is a story that when a traveller in Northumberland was asked by his hostess if he would like a piggy in his bed, he went home and reported that the people up there slept with the pigs for warmth.

pineapple

An odd name for a fruit that has nothing to do with pine-trees or with apples.

But the word 'pineapple' *used* to mean a pine-cone. And if you look up the French for 'pine-cone' you will find that it is *pomme de pin*, 'apple of the pine'.

Pineapples were called pineapples simply because they looked like pine-cones. They took over the word completely, so we had to find a new name for the original 'pineapple'.

What do other countries call pineapples? it seems that they nearly all use a variation of the native Brazilian word: *ananas*.

plonk

Everyone enjoys a glass of 'plonk' – ordinary cheap wine.

The word seems to have originated in the First World War as the soldiers' attempt to pronounce *vin blanc* (white wine). It was used extensively in Australia but now it's a universally-used piece of slang.

Red 'plonk' is therefore something of a contradiction in terms!

plumber

The curious spellings of words often help to point out their origins. Why is there a 'b' in 'plumber'?

Pipes for plumbing were formerly made of lead. The Latin for 'lead' is *plumbum*. Originally, a plumber was a 'lead-worker'.

plunder

Originally this was just an ordinary German word, meaning 'household objects' and was introduced into England at the time of the Civil War by soldiers who had served abroad and who were fighting with Prince Rupert.

poinsettia

It is not often that a diplomat has a flower named after him, but this has happened to Dr. Joel Poinsett (1779-1851), who was American Secretary of War 1837-41. He introduced this lovely plant from Mexico.

An attractive legend concerning the Poinsettia tells of how a little Mexican boy was too poor to give any gifts as he knelt praying one Christmas Eve. He was kneeling outside the church, and when he got up a beautiful red flower began to bloom. The delighted boy immediately placed it in front of the statue of Jesus.

The Mexican name for this flower is *Flor de la Noche Buene* – 'Flower of the Holy Night'.

poodle

Most people think of the poodle as a French dog, but in fact it comes from Germany, where it was used for hunting game in water. It is a *Pudelhund*, or 'puddle-hound', and its name comes from *pudeln*, the German word for 'to splash'. It was originally clipped the way it is in order to help it move in the water.

Our own word, 'puddle', is linked with this.

pope

Papa was a Latin nursery word meaning 'daddy' but came to be used as a respectful name for the bishops of the Western Church. By the fifth century it was restricted to the bishop of Rome, as head of the Church, and in 1073 officially claimed by him. It was he who was to be henceforth *il Papa* or 'the Pope'.

The modern Italian words for 'daddy' and 'Pope' look the same, but *Papa*, 'Pope', is stressed on the first syllable, and *papà*, 'daddy', on the second.

porpoise

Literally, this is a 'pig-fish': its name comes from the two Latin words *porcus*, 'pig', and *piscis*, 'fish'.

posh

When people used to go out to the East and back, the best and most expensive way to travel on board ship was always considered to be '*P*ort *O*ut and *S*tarboard *H*ome'.

The initial letters of these words give us 'posh'!

potato

It seems odd to reflect that no one in England knew about potatoes until the times of Queen Elizabeth I, and even then, only late in her reign.

Sir Walter Raleigh is thought to have brought them back from one of his trips to Virginia about the year 1585: one recent researcher has actually pinpointed the date of the arrival of the first potato into Britain as being 29th July, 1586.

At all events, Sir John Hawkins had already introduced us to the sweet potato, and the name 'potato' derives from the Haitian word for the sweet potato – *batata*.

When it was first introduced, the sweet potato had a fascinating reputation for being a powerful aphrodisiac: Shakespeare knew this when he makes Sir John Falstaff, bursting with lecherous desire in *The Merry Wives of Windsor*, exclaim, 'Let the sky rain potatoes!'

pram

It was surely a very pompous Victorian inventor that could name his new baby-carriage a 'perambulator'. It is derived from Latin *perambulare*, 'to walk about'; in earlier centuries 'perambulator' had meant a person travelling on foot, or a device for measuring distances that was trundled along the ground.

Little wonder it soon became abbreviated to 'pram', a word with a reassuringly sensible and English sound about it.

'Perambulator' might sound absurd, but even absurder was the suggestion of William Barnes, the Dorset clergyman and poet, who was much concerned with languages (he taught himself sixty) and proposed a crazy Anglo-Saxon equivalent: he wanted to call a pram a 'push-wainling'! ('Wainling' is a variant of 'weanling', a baby who is being weaned).

pudding

To most people the name 'pudding' conjures up a cosy picture of delicious food, home cooking, and perhaps above all Christmas dessert.

However, the original meaning of 'pudding' was 'guts' or 'entrails'! When butchers degutted their carcases, all the unwanted rubbish was called 'pudding'. In London, Pudding Lane probably got its name from the filthy droppings from carts taking this kind of rubbish from the butchers in Eastcheap down to the Thames, where they dumped it.

It is interesting to note that the original meaning of 'pudding' is still retained` in the dish known as 'black pudding'.

publican

In the Bible 'publican' means a tax-collector. This was, in Jewish society, someone who gathered the tribute for the hated Roman administration. The frequently-occurring phrase 'publicans and sinners' suggests that these tax-gatherers were a corrupt set of rogues.

Nowadays we use the word to mean an inn-keeper or a keeper of a public house, but in fact this use of the word was originally a rather facetious eighteenth-century joke, perhaps hinting that pub-keepers too were sinners.

The word has gradually gained respectability, and its punning origin has been virtually forgotten.

punch

This drink, made traditionally from five ingredients, spirit, water, sugar, lemon-juice and spice, is said to get its name from the Hindi word, *panch*, and the Sanskrit word, *panca*, which both mean 'five'.

punk

Not many folk will have thought of searching seriously in a dictionary to find the pedigree of this word. But it is worth doing so, for it is not without an interesting history. It was used in North America in the eighteenth century to mean 'rotten wood, fungus growing on wood, used as tinder', and seems to have been so used in Australia and New Zealand too.

By the end of the nineteenth century it could already mean 'something worthless', 'rubbish' – the meanings thought to be at the back of all the modern senses of the word.

pygmy

The interesting thing about the word 'pygmy' is that it is in origin an ancient Greek unit of measurement. The Greeks used the distance from elbow to knuckles as a unit of length – a *pygme* – which worked out at about $13\frac{1}{2}$ inches.

quack

The word 'quack', meaning a medical charlatan or mountebank, is short for 'quacksalver', originally a Dutch word. Dutch *quacken* meant to 'prattle' or 'talk foolishly'. A 'quacksalver' was someone who talked foolishly about his 'salves' or medicines.

quaker

The benign image of Mr. Quaker used as an advertising symbol on packets of cereal presents a contrast to the original Quakers. George Fox, who founded this religious sect, was brought before a magistrate called Bennet in 1650 and reports that "Justice Bennet first called us Quakers because I bid them tremble at the word of the Lord". But these were times of religious fervour, and trembling was a common manifestation of it. Already the name 'Quakers' had been applied by 1647 to a foreign religious sect of women in Southwark.

'Jumpers' was the name given to a group of energetic Welsh Methodists in the eighteenth century, and 'Holy Rollers' and 'Shakers' have been used of several similarly enthusiastic sects.

quandary

Dictionary-makers themselves are in a quandary when it comes to finding the origin of this word. It is first recorded as being used in 1579, and it has been suggested that it comes from a form of 'hypochondria' – 'a morbid state of mind' – or even a garbled form of the French 'Qu'en dirai-je?' – 'What shall I say about it?'

quango

A quango is a '*Qu*asi-*A*utonomous *N*ational *G*overnment *O*rganisation'. These are independent committees which are often today accused of wasting public money.

Once, a British MP claimed that Britain had 372 main quangos, costing in total £11,000 million a year. And he worked out that if all these were one pound notes and laid end to end, they would nearly reach to the moon and back twice!

quarantine

When we put animals or human beings 'in quarantine', they are isolated in order to stop the possible spread of infection. This isolation period, according to the strict meaning of the word, should be 40 days – for the Italian word *quarantina* meant 'a period of forty days'.

query?

The question-mark (?) is really a simplified representation of the letter q, which is short for Latin *quaere*, meaning 'Question this!' *Quaere* became 'query'.

queue

Simply the French for an animal's tail. Forming a queue is 'making a tail'.

The German word for queue is *Schlange*, a 'snake'.

It's odd that the English, who are very good at 'queueing', have no native word for it.

quiz

This seems to have been a word that was just 'thought up' in the late eighteenth century. Its earliest meaning was 'an eccentric person'. Interestingly, another word, 'quoz', meaning the same thing, was invented at about the same time. 'Quiz' also became a verb, meaning 'to tease'.

In the US the word had the meaning 'an oral examination', and it is this sense of it that has become the modern 'question-and-answer contest'.

There is a good story about the origin of the word, that claims it was invented as a result of a bet. An Irish theatre manager called Daly bet a friend, in 1780, that he would introduce a new word into the language within 24 hours.

He won his bet by having this word chalked up on walls all over Dublin and soon everyone was using it and wondering what it meant.

radar

This word is so much a part of our language that we tend to forget that it was originally an acronym for 'radio detection and ranging'.

It was an American expression, and the word 'radar' quickly pushed out the original British term: 'radio-location'.

raglan sleeves

'Raglan' sleeves are named after Lord Raglan (1788-1855), who, when commanding the British troops during the Crimean War wore an overcoat with sleeves that extended over the shoulder to the neckline. He had had his arm amputated (without anaesthetic) after the battle of Waterloo, and perhaps found this style comfortable.

railway

Although railways were a product of the nineteenth century, the word 'rail' has a much longer history, as it comes from the Old French word, *reille*, meaning 'an iron rod'. And this, in turn, came from the Latin word, *regula* – 'a rule'.

Linguistically, 'rail', 'rule' and 'regulation' are all closely linked.

rather

We use the word 'rather' rather a lot.

One of the curiosities of language is the way we can lose vocabulary as well as gain it; the case of 'rather' presents a good example of this phenomenon.

At one time there was a word 'rathe' which meant 'early' or 'soon'. 'Rather', of course, meant 'earlier' or 'sooner', and 'rathest' meant 'earliest' or 'soonest'.

We have kept 'rather', but 'rathe' and rathest' did not really survive beyond the seventeenth century. Which is rather a pity.

recipe

This familiar kitchen word is pure Latin. All it means is 'take': it is the opening instruction for preparing a dish, as in 'take six eggs'.

Incidentally, the medical sign℞ in prescriptions is short for *recipe*, instructing the pharmacist to 'take' the drugs specified, in making up a medicine.

red herring

It used to be believed that if you dragged a dried, smoked herring across the path where a fox had passed, the strong smell would destroy the fox's scent, and so put off the hounds which were pursuing him. Nowadays, a 'red herring' is a tactic to divert people's attention.

rehearsal

This derives from the French word for a 'harrow', which is *herse*. Literally, a rehearsal is a 'harrowing over again' – not the happiest description of the preparations for a concert or a play! *(See **harrowing and hearse**)*

rhinoceros

The first rhinoceros in Europe was brought to King Emmanuel of Portugal in 1513. It must have caused a considerable stir, and Albrecht Dürer, the great German artist, designed a fascinating woodcut of this beast in 1515 from a sketch sent to him from Lisbon.

"It is very well able to defend itself: it has a strong sharp horn towards the end of its nose, which it sets about sharpening when there are stones to hand; it is an animal that comes off best in a fight, for it is the mortal enemy of the elephant." So runs part of the description which is appended to Dürer's woodcut.

And it is this feature which gives the rhino his name: in Greek *rhino-* means 'nose' and *keras* means 'horn'. Literally, then, he is a 'nose-horn'.

rhododendron

A *dendron* is simply the Greek word for a tree; in fact, the study of trees is called 'dendrology' and a tree-expert is known as a 'dendrologist'.

Rhodon means a rose, also in Greek. So a rhododendron is really a 'rose-coloured tree'.

rhubarb

The word 'rhubarb' has a somewhat comical ring, although it would be difficult to say why. Actors, of course, are supposed to keep repeating the word when they are making simulated conversation on stage.

Rha was the Greek word for 'rhubarb' – the name come from the river Rha, the Volga, on whose banks the plant grew profusely. Latin *barbarus*, 'wild' or 'foreign', was added, so that *rhabarbarum*, from which we get 'rhubarb', really means 'foreign rhubarb'.

rigmarole

A curious word, whose first two syllables come from an old term
'ragman', or 'ragment', a catalogue or document, often one with
seals hanging from it. The full word 'rigmarole' is a corruption of
'Ragman Roll'. The Ragman Rolls were the rolls or documents
in which the Scottish king and nobles subscribed their
allegiance to Edward I.

The long lists and tedious terminology contained in these must
have seemed a jumbled mass of incomprehensible nonsense to
ordinary people, and there arose the contemptuous
colloquialism 'rigmarole', meaning a long-winded, rambling
statement or harangue.

rival

The Latin word, *rivus*, means 'river' and so a 'rival' is someone who draws
water from the same stream as yourself.

robin

Our ancestors gave many animals and birds a familiar first name. Some of
these have remained, some have been lost, and some have even taken
over the original name. And this has happened to the robin.

Originally, it was simply called a 'redbreast'. But then, with affection, it
became 'Robin' redbreast.

Nowadays, we simply call this attractive little bird, a *robin*.

An old legend explains that the robin got the red feathers on its breast
when it was trying to pull the thorns out of the crown of Christ, and it
became stained because of the holy blood. (See also, *jackdaw, wren,
magpie* and *martin*)

robot

The word came into English from the Czech play *R.U.R.* (standing for 'Rossum's Universal Robots'), written by Karel Capek in 1921. The Czech word *robota* means 'work' or 'forced labour'. In the play, robots are artificially-made people with mechanical skill but no soul.

When traffic-lights were invented in the 1930s, this word was just beginning to catch on, and for a while traffic-lights were known as 'robots'. They still have the name in South Africa.

rodent

Rats, mice, squirrels: nobody enjoys rodents in his garden. The reason is in their name: *rodens* is the Latin for 'gnawing'. Their prominent incisor teeth make them the perfect gnawers.

sabotage

The word 'sabotage' meaning 'deliberate or malicious damage', comes from French *sabot*, a wooden clog, or, more directly, it is thought, from the verb *saboter*, to clatter with the clogs, to work clumsily, to bungle or damage deliberately.

However, another suggestion is that the original 'saboteurs' were French railway workers who during a strike in 1912 were in the habit of damaging railway lines by removing the *sabots* or 'shoes' that held the lines on to the sleepers.

sadism

Donatien Alphonse François, Comte de Sade, usually known as the Marquis de Sade (1740-1814), a French novelist and dramatist, was the notorious writer of scandalous books who ultimately added the term 'sadism' to our language. He was condemned to death for his wicked sexual practices, but escaped, lived to write his books in prison, and died, mad, in the lunatic asylum at Charenton.

Now rather generally used of the enjoyment of cruelty, 'sadism' was a form of sexual deviation characterised by the desire to inflict pain: it is described by de Sade, who apparently had this tendency himself.

salary

This word derived from Latin *salarium*, originally the 'salt allowance' paid to Roman soldiers. In Roman times, salt was much more precious than it is today, because of the difficulties of obtaining and transporting it. Embedded like a fossil in the word 'salary' is this odd fact of history.

salmon

If you have ever seen a salmon leaping up a weir with extraordinary force and energy, you will not be surprised to hear that the name 'salmon' is connected with the Latin word *salire*, to leap. The Latin name of the fish, *salmo*, meant 'the leaper'.

salute

When you greet someone you often ask how he is and wish him good health. *Salute* simply comes from the Latin word for health and safety. It then came to mean the greeting itself, and then the action of greeting, which has become a formal drill in the armed services.

sandwich

Sandwiches are so commonplace that it seems amazing that they actually had to be 'invented'! It is said that they were first used and popularised by the fourth Earl of Sandwich (1718-1792), who was so keen on gambling that he could not bear to waste time on eating proper meals.

Incidentally, the town of Sandwich is in Kent, quite close to a village named Ham. An intriguing sign in Kent can be seen pointing to 'Ham Sandwich'.

San Francisco

There was, in the twelfth century, an Italian boy called Giovanni, whose father, Pietro Bernardone, was a rich merchant. The father did a lot of trade in France, and hoped his son would continue expanding the business in that country. Accordingly, so it is said, he taught his son French, dressed him in French clothes and nicknamed him 'Francesco', 'the little Frenchman'.

But the boy never went into his father's business. When he grew up, he turned instead to helping and protecting the poor and sick. But he kept the nickname his father had given him. He was none other than Saint Francis of Assisi.

In the late eighteenth century the Spanish established a colony in California and set up a mission there in his name; the Spanish for Saint Francis is *San Francisco*.

sanguine

Today this word means 'optimistic', or even 'over-optimistic', but it used to mean 'having a preponderance of blood in the body' from the medieval idea that your character depended on the proportions in which four liquids or 'humours' were mixed inside you.

One of these 'humours' was blood (Latin *sanguis*) and if it predominated in the mixture, you would be courageous, confident, and amorous – and of course have a ruddy complexion, the traditional sign of a cheerful disposition. (See **humour**)

Saturday

This day of the week gets its name from the Roman God Saturn. The Old English name *Saeternesdaeg* was a translation of the Latin name for the day, *Saturni dies*.

scientist

The invention of a new word often marks a step in the history of human thought, or an advance in technology, and yet sometimes an idea can exist well before someone comes up with the right word for it.

Rather surprisingly, the word 'scientist' was not thought up until as late as 1840, when a Cambridge philosopher, William Whewell, in his *Philosophy of Inductive Sciences*, wrote: "We need very much a name to describe a cultivator of science in general. I should incline to call him a *scientist*". In the same book, Whewell also invented the word 'physicist'.

The nearest equivalent to the word 'scientist' up to that time was 'natural philosopher'. Francis Bacon, writing *The Advancement of Learning* in 1605, struggled to find new words for his ideas, but many never survived: *contristation, digladiation, morigeration, redargution, ventosity . . .*

scout

Why is a scout called a scout?

Because he is trained to use his *ears*!

The French for 'listen' is *écouter*, and the word 'scout' is derived from an earlier form of this, *escouter*. Since a scout is someone who is sent out to spy, he must keep his ears open as well as his eyes.

schizophrenia

If you suffer from 'schizophrenia' you are the victim of having a split mind. The word comes the two Greek words, *skhizein*, to split, and *phren*, a mind.

Nineteenth century quack doctors thought up a phoney science which they called 'phrenology' which was supposed to tell you your character according to the bumps on your head!

scuba diving

As with other acronyms, such as 'Pakistan' and 'laser', we tend to accept 'scuba' as a word in its own right, not realising that it is a collection of initial letters.

In case landlubbers need to be reminded of it, 'scuba' is, more lengthily, a self-contained underwater breathing apparatus.

secretary

An obvious one this, but not always remembered – that a secretary is someone who can be trusted to keep secrets.

The original Latin, from which we get the word, 'secret' means something that is 'not seen' or, *se - cretus*.

September

Before January and February were introduced into the Roman calendar a few centuries before the birth of Christ, September used to be the seventh month of the year. The Latin for 'seven' is *septem*, which gave the month its name.

sherry

What possible connection can there be between Julius Caesar and a glass of sherry?

The old name for sherry, *sherris*, represents a sixteenth-century pronunciation of the Spanish town from which it came – Jerez. 'Sherris' sounded like a plural, so the singular 'sherry' evolved. Jerez itself was once called Xeres, which, according to some, was a distorted form of *Caesaris*. The name of the town, long ago, was thought to have been *Caesaris urbs*, or 'City of Caesar'.

shilling

With the decimalisation of our coinage in 1971, several coins and names of coins became obsolete, and may soon be forgotten about. You still hear traditionalists calling a five-penny piece a 'shilling' or even a 'bob' – but many of today's schoolchildren do not know that it used to be worth twelve old pennies.

The word 'shilling' is Anglo-Saxon and older. It used to be *scilling*, and is of very uncertain origin. Some think it comes from a word-stem meaning 'to ring or resound'; others connect it with a stem that means 'to split or divide', and refer to the medieval practice of using gold and silver arm-bands in place of coins. A 'scilling' is thought to have been a measured-off segment of such an arm-band; it was equal to twelve 'penings' (pennies).

shrapnel

General Henry Shrapnel shares with his older contemporary Monsieur Guillotin the dubious honour of having his name linked in perpetuity with the destruction of the human body.

His family actually asked that his invention be named after him. As an officer in the Royal Artillery he invented in about 1793 a shell that came to be known as 'spherical case shot', consisting of a thin, fused, outer casing containing musket balls, and a charge that was enough to burst the casing in mid-flight and release the musket balls, which careered onwards and outwards, causing terrible wounds. When he died in 1842, his family would have liked to put up a monument to him, but could not afford to, so they asked that the spherical case shot should be renamed 'shrapnel shell' instead.

Shrove Tuesday

The eating of pancakes on Shrove Tuesday is the only Shrovetide custom that is still widely practised.

This day is the one before Ash Wednesday, the beginning of Lent. During the forty days of Lent, people commemorated Jesus's fasting in the wilderness by doing without certain foods themselves. As a part of the preparation for this fast they would go, during the three days of Shrovetide, to confess their sins and be pardoned. This was to be 'shriven' and when the priest 'shrove' them, they were ready for Lent.

Shrove Tuesday, the last of the three days, was a day of merrymaking; the eating of pancakes had a practical reason in that pancakes used up the fat and eggs that were to be prohibited during Lent.

sideburns

These hairy masculine ornaments are named after General Ambrose Burnside (died 1881), Federal commander of the army of the Potomac in the American Civil War. His extensive side-whiskers became famous and fashionable, though the two halves of his name have become oddly transposed during the course of time.

silhouette

Étienne de Silhouette (1709-1767), French Minister of Finance in 1759, is said to have been so mean in his attempts to save money that the cheap 'silhouette' type of portrait, an outlined profile filled in with black, gets its name from his tight-fistedness. Another explanation of the word is that he made 'silhouettes' himself, and another, that, as a minister, he was so incompetent that the phrase *à la silhouette* came into use meaning 'clumsily', 'inefficiently', hence 'incompletely' – the silhouette being considered an incomplete sort of portrait.

silly

This word has an honourable origin. It used to be 'seely' and comes from the Old English word *saelig*, which meant 'blessed' or 'innocent'. Modern German has the word in the form *selig*, meaning 'blessed'. Over the years 'silly' has changed its meaning, so that it is now an abusive term. The development in sense seems to have gone like this: 'blessed' – 'innocent' – 'helpless' – 'lowly' – 'simple' – 'foolish'. In old hymns and carols you sometimes find the word used in an earlier sense, as in the line. "Behold a silly tender babe".

snob

In lists of college students many years ago, the entry S.NOB. was put against those who were *sine nobilitate* or 'without nobility'. Also, Cambridge students used the word to describe the townsfolk of Cambridge.

Presumably those who were 'snobs' and lacked noble birth sometimes tried hard to imitate those who were noblemen.

snot

You may quail at the sight of this word, but it is well over a thousand years old – it existed in Old English, and is even now to be found in Danish and Dutch. In the seventeenth century it was the normal term for what is now politely referred to by its respectable-sounding Latin name, *mucus*.

English tends to begin nose-connected words with 'sn'. There are, to name just a few, 'sneeze', 'sniff', 'snore', 'snort', 'snout' – and the dictionary will yield many more!

sorry

This is related to the word 'sore' rather than to the word 'sorrow'.

'Sore' comes from the Old English word *sar*, 'pain, wound', and 'sorry' from the adjective formed from *sar: sarig*. In the past 'sore' was used as an adverb meaning originally 'painfully' but later just 'extremely' or 'very'. We find it in the archaic expression 'sore afraid'. German *sehr*, 'very', is closely related to 'sore'. It, too, means literally 'painfully'.

spade

This is the basic digging tool, and as you can imagine, the origin of its name goes back a long way.

The Old English word was *spadu*, and this is linked with a Greek word, *spathe*, meaning a 'broad blade'.

The Spanish word *espade*, meaning 'sword', also comes from this Greek word, and it is interesting to see that on Spanish playing-cards the 'spades' are in fact shaped like swords – and our own playing-card 'spade' derives its name from this.

In fact, the dual possibilities of using a flat-shaped piece of metal for warfare as well as for cultivating the ground are memorably summed up in the well-known biblical phrase 'swords into ploughshares'.

spaniel

The name of this dog is no more than the French word for 'Spanish'. Its old French name was *espaignol* or *espaigneul*.

The modern French word for 'Spaniard' is *Espagnol*, and 'spaniel' is now *épagneul*. The dog originally came from Spain and was used as a hunting dog in medieval times.

spelling-bee

Why *bee*?

Since a bee symbolises industry and social co-operation, the Americans adopted the word to mean a social gathering for some useful work, and were using it with this meaning as early as the beginning of the last century. You could attend a sewing-bee, or a quilting-bee or various kinds of outdoor 'bees' that involved helping with the harvest, fruit-picking, etc.

A 'spelling-bee' is a gathering of people to compete in a spelling competition – an activity whose social usefulness some might question.

sport

The Old French verb *se desporter*, interpreted literally, means 'to take oneself off', or 'to carry oneself away', but what it really meant was 'to stop what one is doing and divert or amuse oneself' – in other words, to 'take oneself off' from one's serious occupation. *Desporter* became 'disport' in English, and the 'di' dropped off, giving us 'sport'.

squirrel

What you notice most about a squirrel is its tail, and it is this feature that gives it its name.

The word 'squirrel' comes through medieval French *esquireul* (the modern French *écureuil*) from the Greek word for 'squirrel', *skiouros*. *Skiouros* is composed of two words – *skia*, 'shadow', and *oura*, 'tail', so a squirrel is a 'shadow-tail'.

strike

Why should workers, when they stop work as a protest, go 'on strike'? In French they go *en grève* (La Grève was the bank of the Seine where dissatisfied workers assembled) and in German they go *in den Ausstand* ('standing-out'), or *in den Streik* (borrowing the English word). So there is no common international thread.

The term 'strike' seems to have come from the nautical 'strike' found in expressions such as 'to strike sail', meaning 'to take down or dismantle the sails'.

To 'strike work', 'strike tools' or just 'strike' – in other words to put down your tools and refuse to work, are uses that seem to come in along with the industrial revolution, about the beginning of the nineteenth century.

subtle

The Latin word from which this comes, *subtilis*, was originally a weaving term meaning 'fine in texture', from *sub tela*, 'under the warp'. So it is the fineness of the weaver's art that is being recalled in the word 'subtle'.

sundae

It seems to be generally agreed that 'sundae', the ice-cream dish served with fruit, nuts and syrup, is a variation on 'Sunday', but no-one quite knows what Sunday had to do with it.

One story, probably apocryphal, goes like this: at one time a law in the American state of Virginia prohibited the sale of soda-fountain drinks on a Sunday. One imaginative café-owner sidestepped this officious law by thickening such a drink with fruit and ice-cream, so that it turned, legally, into a meal! This 'Sunday drink' was entitled a 'Sundae'.

Sunday

It seems to be only in the Germanic languages that this day retains its dedication to the sun. The name is a translation of the Roman name, *dies solis* – the 'day of the sun', and is paralleled by German *Sonntag*, Dutch *zondag*, Swedish *söndag*.

But French *dimanche* is a contraction of ecclesiastical Latin *dies dominica*, 'day of the Lord', and Italian *domenica* and Spanish *domingo* just use *dominica* from the Latin name.

swastika

The name of this symbol adopted by the Nazis comes from the ancient Indian literary language, Sanskrit – the language from which, for instance, **juggernaut** comes.

The Sanskrit name for this 'good-luck' symbol, *svastika*, is from *svasti*, 'well-being'.

sycophant

'An apple for the teacher'!

A 'sycophant' is used nowadays to mean someone who tries desperately to curry favour, or someone who is always trying hard to please.

Its strange derivation is from the Greek words *sykon*, a fig, and *phainein*, to show. It may well be that the original 'sycophants' were those who brought figs, not apples, as a gift for their superiors.

symposium

The modern symposium, a serious debate by serious people on matters of importance, started life somewhat disreputably as a Greek drinking-party (from *syn*, 'with', and *posis*, 'drinking'). But even the Greek symposium was not always altogether frivolous; sometimes the drinkers would send away the flute-girls and entertain themselves with conversation instead – as happens most notably in Plato's dialogue, *The Symposium*, where the philosopher Socrates, the wild political adventurer Alcibiades, and the comic poet Aristophanes, all get down to discussing the subject of love.

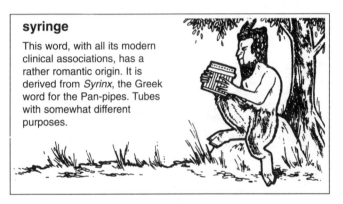

syringe

This word, with all its modern clinical associations, has a rather romantic origin. It is derived from *Syrinx*, the Greek word for the Pan-pipes. Tubes with somewhat different purposes.

tabby

The word 'tabby' has an interesting past. It derives from the name of a suburb of Baghdad – Attabiy (whose name came from a prince called Attab) – where they used to make a special kind of silk taffeta with markings much the same as those of our 'tabby' cats. From the name of this suburb came the medieval French word *atabis*, a name for the fabric itself; it became shortened to *tabis* and came into English as 'tabby', a striped or plain taffeta, or a taffeta with a watered or waved pattern on it. People started referring to striped cats as 'tabby-cats'.

tadpole

The 'pole' part comes from our old word 'poll', meaning 'head'. At election times we have 'polling' stations when we 'go to the poll' – which is really another way of saying we are 'counting heads'.

And the 'tad' part is a relic of our Saxon name for a toad, *tade* or *tadie*.

In medieval times tadpoles were known as 'pollwyggles', and a number of similar words are used in dialect: pollywog, polliwig, porwiggle, etc. (See *toad*).

tandem

A joke word. Latin *tandem* means 'at length'. Some wit once called the arrangement of having two horses harnessed to a vehicle one behind the other a 'tandem' because they were 'at length' and when later the bicycle for two was invented this also became known as a 'tandem'.

tank

When the army tank was first invented by the British in the First World War it was known, for secrecy, as a 'water-carrier for Mesopotamia' – this was just an arbitrary code-name, but the workmen manufacturing it took the name up literally, and called it 'that tank thing' in reference to the term 'water-carrier'. The inventor himself, Sir Ernest Swinton, then suggested adopting the word 'tank'.

SCHUTZENGRABENVERNICHTUNGSAPPARAT

Hitler wanted a nice German-based word to replace the English word 'tank'. But the suggested replacement – 'Schutzengrabenvernichtungsapparat – somehow didn't quite catch on!

tantalise

The old Greek legend told of Tantalus, the son of Zeus, who was punished for his crimes by having to stand up to his chin in water with fruit hanging over his head. He was desperately hungry and thirsty, but the fruit was pulled away from him when he looked up and the waters receded when he stooped to drink. In this way, he was 'tantalised'.

tarantella

This is familiar as the name for a piece of music; it was originally the name of a type of dance.

The word is connected with the poisonous spider, the 'tarantula'. There was a kind of nervous disorder common in Southern Italy between the fifteenth and seventeenth centuries which was somehow linked up with frenzied dancing; whether the dancing was a symptom of, or cure for, the disease is not certain. The disease was called 'tarantism' and was attributed to the bite of the tarantula. The energetic dance called a 'tarantella' is reputed to have been devised as a cure for tarantism.

The spider, the dance, and the disease, get their names from Taranto, in Southern Italy, where the spider is common.

tarmac

The Gaelic prefix 'mac' meaning 'son of', found in Scottish and Irish surnames, forms the second syllable of 'tarmac' – a new twist of meaning given to it that makes inventor John McAdam an emulator of Charles Macintosh.

John McAdam, born at Ayr in 1756, so successfully experimented with road-construction that in 1815 he was appointed surveyor-general of roads in Britain. He set about 'macadamizing' roads as widely as he could. His method was to cover the earthen base with a layer of irregularly broken stones, and allow these to become pressed down into the surface by the wheeled traffic using the road, before adding a layer of smaller stones, and so on.

When cars were invented, many years after McAdam's death, a new technique had to be developed, using tar to bind the stones, and the new type of surfacing became known as tarmacadam, or 'tarmac' for short.

tattoo

The military word 'tattoo', meaning a 'drumbeat', has an interesting past. Originally it was a drumbeat signal to landlords in taverns to stop serving drinks and for soldiers to return from the taverns to their quarters. The word comes from Dutch *taptoe*, 'tap-to' or 'closing the taps' (of barrels), which became 'taptoo' in English. The military entertainment held in the evening is an elaboration of this 'drumbeat at night'.

As for the other meaning of 'tattoo' – the marking of patterns on skin – this is a Polynesian word from the South Sea Islands.

taunt

The word 'taunt', meaning to reproach or censure in a biting, sarcastic manner, could come from the Old French *tanter*, to tempt, or else, more interestingly, from the French *tant pour tant*, in English 'tit for tat'.

tawdry

A popular autumn fair used to be held at Ely in honour of the patron saint of the town, St. Audrey (the name was originally Etheldrida or Aethelthryth), daughter of a king of East Anglia. St. Audrey died of a throat tumour, which she considered a punishment for having worn jewelled necklaces as a girl. In memory of her death, a woman's silk necktie known as 'a tawdry-lace' (a corrupted form of 'St. Audrey's lace') was traditionally sold at the fair.

In *The Winter's Tale* (IV, 3, 252), Shakespeare's character Mopsa says "Come, you promised me a tawdry-lace and a pair of sweet gloves". The quality of the tawdry-lace and other trinkets bought at the fair probably declined over the years, and the adjective 'tawdry' came into use meaning 'showy but worthless'.

taxi

At first these were referred to as 'taxi-cabs' and this word, believe it nor not, was the shortened term for 'taximeter-cabriolet' – the grand name for a public vehicle which was fitted with a meter to register the 'tax' or fare. The word, 'tax', itself is linked with 'task', as being a burden which is imposed upon someone.

teddy-bear

Bears seem to fascinate creators of film and fiction for children. Pooh, Paddington, Rupert, Yogi: they all have their own followers. But the bear to start the bear-craze off was a little cub whose life, apparently, was spared by the American President Theodore ('Teddy') Roosevelt, when he was hunting in Mississippi in 1902.

The story reached the newspapers and featured in popular cartoons. A Brooklyn shopkeeper and his wife began to make stuffed toy bears, and got permission from the President to call them 'Teddy-bears'. They quickly became all the rage not only in the USA but also in Britain.

teetotal

Everyone knows that a 'teetotal' person is one who abstains totally from drinking intoxicating drinks, but the 'tee' may well leave you guessing.

A generally accepted explanation is that it was prefixed by way of emphasis to 'total' by Richard Turner of Preston, who produced the word in 1833 in a speech advocating abstinence.

A more imaginative tradition makes Richard Turner a stammerer who had difficulty in saying 'total'.

'Tee-totally', as an emphatic form of 'totally', was apparently known as an Irish colloquialism as early as 1829.

telly

The 'tele' in 'television' is in origin a rather rare and poetic Greek prefix meaning 'at a distance' or 'afar off'. The television is such a central feature in our homes that it is not surprising that the word should have been shortened to 'telly' – with the result that this small word from ancient Greek has acquired a major new significance in the technologically advanced life of the twentieth century.

tennis

Tennis began in France, and the name is a version of the French word *Tenez!*, 'Hold it!' or 'See what you can do with that!'

on tenterhooks

A 'tenter' was a wooden frame used to stretch cloth during its manufacture. The cloth was fastened to the frame by hooks called 'tenterhooks'.

If you are 'on tenterhooks' you are being stretched taut like the cloth and are in an agony, in fact, of suspense.

test

The verb, 'to test', comes from the old medieval alchemists, who used to try out various substances in a pot, or *testa*. The word, *testa*, itself came from the Latin word for 'a head' because it was round and head-shaped. The French get their word *la tête* from this, too.

The meaning of 'test', therefore, shifted from the thing itself, the pot, to the action you did with it – trying out or examining.

tethera-bumpit

Here is a word few people are likely to have encountered. It comes from the set of numerals that have been particularly associated with counting sheep in various parts of the country. Here is 1-20 in this counting system: Clearly there is a similarity between these numbers and their Welsh equivalents. It is thought they were probably introduced into England in recent centuries by groups of Welsh speakers.

1. Yan	11. Yan-a-dik
2. Tan	12. Tan-a-dik
3. Tethera	13. Tethera-dik
4. Pethera	14. Pethera-dik
5. Pimp	15. Bumpit
6. Sethera	16. Yan-a-bumpit
7. Lethera	17. Tan-a-bumpit
8. Hovera	18. Tethera-bumpit
9. Covera	19. Pethera-bumpit
10. Dik	20. Figgit

thug

The original 'thugs' were members of an Indian religious sect, finally suppressed in the nineteenth century, who practised 'thuggee' or the strangling and robbing of human victims as a sacred rite to the goddess Kali.

The word comes from Hindi *thag*, a swindler.

Thursday

This day is dedicated to the Norse god, Thor (or his Anglo-Saxon equivalent Thunor) – the thunderer – who was second only to Odin (or Woden) among the gods of Northern Europe. The Romans called this day after Jupiter or Jove, who was also their god of thunder. The Latin name for Thursday was *Jovis dies*, 'day of Jove', and it is from this that the French *jeudi* and Italian *giovedì* are derived.

toad

Many legends and superstitions surround toads, including the astonishing former belief that larks and toads exchange eyes. And there was a lingering belief in the 'toadstone', inside its head, which would cure any pain or venomous hurt.

But they are harmless and interesting creatures and St. Patrick need not have cursed them out of Ireland, as he is alleged to have done.

The collective noun is a 'knot' of toads, and its name goes back into Saxon times, when they were called *tades*, or *tadies*. (See **tadpole**)

tomato

Just like the sweet potato, the tomato came from South America, and when it was first introduced to European countries it was considered to be a strong aphrodisiac. Even today the Germans have the word *Liebesapfel*, or 'love-apple' for the tomato.

There is a curious word-history behind this belief. It was known as *pomo dei moro* (apple of the Moors) by the Italians: but then the French turned this into *pomme d'amour*. In England too they became known as 'love-apples'.

The actual name 'tomato' derives from native Mexican word *tomatl*.

tory

Astonishing, 'tories' originally meant outlawed Irish bog-trotters! The term goes back to the time of Oliver Cromwell. It is an English version of an Irish word meaning 'to pursue': presumably, as robbers they pursued their victims.

The word was too good to lose, so its next use was to refer in a damning way to the Stuart supporters of Bonnie Prince Charlie. Later, it came to suggest upholders of traditional authority. Thus their opponent 'Whigs', or 'Whiggamores', were considered rebels.

tradescantia

If you go to Hatfield House, just north of London, in Hertfordshire, you will see a carving on the Grand Staircase of one of the greatest gardeners of all time – John Tradescant.

John Tradescant was head gardener to (among others) Robert Cecil, 1st Earl of Salisbury, and Charles I. He travelled thousands of miles, to Holland, Flanders, Russia and Algeria in search of new plants. His son, John Tradescant the younger, succeeded him at Charles I's palace at Oatlands, Surrey. The younger Tradescant also travelled for plants, making three visits to North America.

Among the plants the two men introduced into England are lupins, Michaelmas daisies, Virginia creeper, and, of course, the popular houseplant that comes from America and bears their name, 'Tradescantia'.

treacle

It's rather difficult to see what connection this could have with the Greek word from which it comes, meaning 'antidote to a poisonous bite', or, more liberally translated, 'viper's flesh'! But the history of the word 'treacle' goes like this. *Theriake* was the Greek term for an antidote to a bite from a *therion*, a 'wild beast' or a 'poisonous beast', and it was believed that the best antidote to a viper's poison was a medicine made up using the viper's own flesh. *Theriake* turned into Latin *theriaca*, and probably a later form *triaca*, before coming into English as 'treacle'.

'Treacle' came to mean any antidote or sovereign remedy. The sweet syrup extracted during sugar-refining came to be used as a palatable medium in which to mix the medicine, and, finally, the name 'treacle' attached itself to this syrup.

trivial

This means, literally, 'belonging to the place where three roads meet'. It comes from Latin *trivium*, which meant originally a fork in the road, a meeting of three roads, or a cross-roads, and later a public street, square or highway. But the life and talk of the public streets was banal, commonplace and unimportant – in a word, 'trivial'.

troglodyte

This odd word comes from two Greek words, *trogle*, meaning a cave, and *duein*, meaning to enter. So it really means 'something which has entered a cave'.

The Greeks called any primitive cave-dwellers 'troglodytes', and one Roman writer, Pliny, wrote that they ate snakes. (Surprisingly, see **wren**).

trout

Just as the salmon is the 'leaping fish', getting its name from the Latin word for 'to jump', so the trout is the 'greedy gnawing fish', its name coming from the Greek word, *troktes*, 'the gnawer', from *trogein*, to gnaw.

Tuesday

Like the other days of the week, 'Tuesday' is Anglo-Saxon. Its name used to be *Tiewsdaeg*, the day of Tiw, who was the god of war. The Romans also honoured Mars, their war-god, on this day, and called it *Martis dies*, the day of Mars.
Italian *martedì* and French *mardi* come from this Latin form.

tulip

When tulips were first brought to Europe in the sixteenth century, they caused tremendous excitement, the bulbs changing hands for quite extortionate prices.

The flowers came from Turkey, and it was from the Turkish word, *tulband* or *tuliband*, turban, that our own word 'tulip' was derived. It is its turban-like shape that gives the flower its name.

turkey

Why are turkeys called turkeys?

Because, in a way, they came from Turkey. 'Turkey' or 'turkey-cock' was a name for the guinea-fowl of Africa, because, so it is said, it was exported through Turkey to this country. When a similar type of bird was found in America, it was also called a 'turkey'. The modern 'turkey' is the American one. In France the guinea-fowl or pintade of Abyssinia was called *poule d'Inde*, 'hen of India'; *d'Inde* became *dinde*, a feminine word, and finally the masculine word *dindon* was devised and, like 'turkey', the name was transferred to the American bird.

tweed

This is woollen, twilled (two-threaded) fabric. A batch was sent to London from Scotland in 1829 labelled *tweal*, in almost illegible hand-writing. It was misread as 'tweed' and this has been its name ever since.

tweezers

The derivation of this work is perhaps odder than the word itself would suggest.

The French for 'case' is *étui*. The word was used in English, spelt 'etui', 'etwee', or 'twee', and it referred to a case containing small instruments: these could be a surgeon's instruments, or small things such as needles, thimbles, scissors, etc.

Because there were several instruments in the case, the plural 'etuis' became used for it, sometimes spelt 'etweese', but often 'tweeze'. The instruments became known as 'tweezes' or sometimes 'a pair (meaning 'a set') of tweezes'. 'Tweezes' became lengthened to 'tweezers', and 'a pair of tweezers' began to mean the little pincers (used for instance, for plucking eyebrows or picking up tiny objects) that were originally included among the instruments inside an 'étui'.

umbrella

This comes from the Italian word *ombrella* or *ombrello*, which literally means 'a little shade' (from Latin *umbra*, 'shade'). We think of the umbrella as a protection against rain of course, but strictly speaking, it is a protection against sun or rain. Dr. Johnson in his dictionary defines it as "a skreen used in hot countries to keep off the sun, and in others to bear off the rain". The French words for 'umbrella' and 'sunshade', *parapluie*, meaning 'against the rain' and *parasol* (borrowed into English), meaning 'against the sun' seem to have got things sorted out more appropriately.

umpire

An umpire was originally an arbitrator between disputing parties. Because he himself was not one of those involved in the dispute, he was a 'non-equal' or 'non-peer'. This is just how he gets his name.

It is the Old French *nonper*, *non* meaning 'not' and *per* (modern French *pair*, English 'peer'), meaning 'equal'. The word used to be 'a noumpere' in English but the 'n' became attached to 'a', and it turned into 'an umpire'.

For a word that gained rather than lost an 'n', see *nickname*.

union jack

Why 'Jack'?

The word 'jack' can denote an article that is smaller than the standard size; the 'jack' bowl in the game of bowls is an instance; in the case of flags flown by warships the jack is smaller than the ensign, and is fastened to the jackstaff, in the bows.

In 1606, a few years after the union of the crowns of Scotland and England under James I (James VI of Scotland), a 'union' flag was designed, combining the cross of St. Andrew with the cross of St. George. In 1801, at the union with Ireland, the cross of St. Patrick was added to the design. The 'union jack' is a small version of this 'union flag', and there is no good reason why the name should be applied in general to the national flag, but the popular name has stuck.

utopia

This word, the title of a book by Sir Thomas More published in 1516, was a name invented by him for an imaginary island in which there dwelt a perfect society.

It is made up from two Greek words, *ou*, 'not', and *topos*, 'place'. So 'utopia' really means 'nowhere'. A sad comment by Sir Thomas on the hopes of statesmen and politicians!

vaccination

A word that you associate more with hygienic surgeries than with cows. But the term derives from Latin *vacca*, cow. Edward Jenner, in the eighteenth century, learnt that milkmaids who had caught cowpox from cows (cowpox was a mild type of smallpox) became immune to smallpox itself, a disfiguring and often-fatal disease. He argued that inoculation with the cowpox virus would make the inoculated person form anti-bodies to this 'vaccine' that would be effective against the smallpox virus. The eventual result of his work was universal 'vaccination' and thus universal protection against smallpox. The word is now used generally of inoculation with a mild virus that will give immunity against a more dangerous one.

valentine

It would be satisfying to find some connection between St. Valentine and the traditional romantic practices associated with his day; but, alas, there is none whatever.

It seems, in fact, that there are two St. Valentines who have their feast-day on 14 February: one was a priest in Rome who was clubbed to death in the year 269; the other was a bishop of the city of Terni who was martyred in Rome. The sending of valentines and other St. Valentine's day customs may have their origin in the Roman festival of Lupercalia, held in mid-February in honour of the god Pan, at which rites to secure fertility for the flocks, and for women, too, were practised; alternatively there may be some connection with the medieval tradition that birds began to mate on 14 February.

vampire

The word 'vampire' is Hungarian, but the word is used throughout all the Slavonic languages – Russian, Polish, Czech, Bulgarian, etc. And, through these, it has entered into all the various European languages.

It first came to England in 1734 in a book called *Travels of Three Gentlemen* in the sentence: "These Vampyres are supposed to be bodies of deceased Persons animated by Evil Spirits, which come out of the Graves, in the Night time, suck the Blood of many of the Living, and thereby destroy them."

The word was used as a zoological term first in 1774 – forty years later, so this means that the biologist got the word from the superstition, and not the other way round.

vaseline®

This word was deliberately fabricated by an American, Robert A. Cheseborough, in 1872, as a tradename for soft petroleum jelly.

He took the first syllable from the German word for water (*Wasser*, pronounced 'vasser') giving 'vas'. Then he joined this to the first syllable of the Greek word for oil (*elaion*) producing 'vasel'. Then he rounded the whole thing off with the scientific ending '-ine'. Hence: 'Vaseline'.

ventriloquism

Whoever invented the word 'ventriloquism' must have been taken in by the whole process. Quite literally, it means 'belly-talk', and comes from the two words, *venter*, meaning a belly, and *loquor* meaning to speak.

Of course, ventriloquists don't talk from the stomachs, so it is a rather odd word.

veronica

The speedwell genus is given the name Veronica, after St. Veronica, a woman of Jerusalem who gave Jesus a handkerchief to wipe his face when he was on the way to Calvary.

The story goes that after Jesus had wiped his face he returned the piece of cloth to her, and a perfect likeness of his face was found to be imprinted on it.

The cloth became known as the Vera Icon, or 'True Likeness' and the woman became known as Veronica.

violet

The genus Viola is named directly from the Latin *viola*, so the name goes back for thousands of years. Francis Bacon, in his *Essays*, wrote: 'That which above all others yields the sweetest smell in the air is the violet'.

When Napoleon was banished to the island of Elba he boasted that he would return with the violets. He thus became known as 'Corporal Violet' among his supporters, who would greet one another with the meaningful question: 'Do you like violets?' (The correct answer, if you did support him, was supposed to be 'Eh bien!')

There is an enormous amount of symbolism and significance surrounding this little flower, which was the symbol of the ancient city of Athens.

In Christian times it has come to signify love, truth, and faithfulness.

villain

This word has come a long way since its original meaning, which was simply a slave who worked in a country house, or 'villa': in other words, he was someone who held a low position in life.

vinegar

This is wine *'vin'* that is sour *'aigre'* – both words, of course, are French. Our word, 'eager', meaning 'keen', is the same as this French word, *aigre*, and so when you are 'eager' you are said to have the same sharpness as vinegar has on the tongue.

viper

Many snakes lay eggs, but adders do not; they bring forth their young alive. And the fact that they do this gives them their alternative name – 'viper'.

The Latin word *vipera*, viper, was contracted from *vivipera*, which comes from two words: *vivus*, alive, and *parere*, to give birth to.

volume

This word takes us back to the ancient world when books were written on rolls or scrolls of papyrus, which you had to read by winding and unwinding. The Latin word *volumen*, from which it comes, means literally 'something wound up' from the verb *volvere*, to roll or wind.

The bound book or 'codex' began to take over from the scroll in early Christian times – but the inappropriate name 'volume' was used for it. The other meaning of 'volume' – mass or capacity, seems to come originally from the dimensions or 'bulk' of a book.

water butt

The Latin word *butta* gave rise to a number of words meaning 'bottle' in several languages: our own *bottle*, the French *bouteille*, the Spanish *botella*, and so on.

'Butt' is one of these bottle-words. We have butts of all sizes to collect water in our gardens, but in the wine trade a 'butt' is a precise measure of 126 gallons if it contains wine; but a precise measure of 108 gallons if it contains beer or sherry.

Wednesday

It may be many centuries since the Anglo-Saxons worshipped the pagan god Woden, but it is his name that is preserved in 'Wednesday'. He was the equivalent of the great Scandinavian god Odin, the chief of the Northern European deities.

So 'Wednesday' is 'Woden's Day'. Its spelling comes from the Old English form *Wodnesdaeg*. Woden was identified with the Roman god Mercury. The Latin name for the day, *Mercurii dies* became French *mercredi* and Italian *mercoledi*.

wellies

Children love to splash about in 'wellies' and gardeners use them a great deal, but not many remember the great Duke of Wellington, the 'Iron Duke', who made this type of footwear popular.

He wore his boots as he conquered Napoleon at the battle of Waterloo, and his fame and popularity naturally made him a trend-setter with his 'wellington' boots.

It's curious to think that long after the Duke of Wellington has passed into the history books, his name is still alive – and kicking!

whisky

Whisky is 'the water of life'. The word comes from Gaelic *uisgebeatha*, formed from *uisge*, water, and *beatha*, life. It is interesting to see how 'water of life' turns up in various languages as a name for spirits: *aqua vitae* was the medieval alchemists' Latin name for unrefined alcohol; from this comes *akvavit*, Scandinavian schnaps; and in French we find *eau-de-vie*, brandy.

whitsun

Whit Sunday, or White Sunday, was called by this name because at this time converts to the primitive church used to wear white robes.
Children at christenings as well as at confirmation used to wear white, as a symbol of purity, carrying on the tradition of 'candidates' (see **candidate**) in ancient Rome.

window

The origin of this word is to be found in two Old Norse words, *vindr*, which means 'wind', and *auga*, meaning an 'eye'. A *vindauga* was literally a 'wind-eye' or an opening through which you could get fresh air. It was not until the fifteenth century or so that glass became common in the windows of ordinary dwelling-houses.

woodpecker

The origin of the name is self-evident. He 'pecks' (a form of 'picks') the wood; and in French he is *un pic*.

The beautifully expressive dialect word, not used often enough, is a 'yaffle', which comes from its distinctive laughing cry.

And it was Tennyson who conjured up the rather absurd 'yaffingale', probably thinking of 'nightingale' when he invented it.

worship

When you 'worship' God you are really considering God's 'worth': you are giving praise to his 'worth-ship' or 'worthiness' – an explanation that helps to make sense of the strange title 'His Worship the Mayor'.

wren

Although we may be vaguely familiar with the name, we do not often hear people calling the wren 'Jenny' wren nowadays.

At one time 'Jenny' was a common name given to the wren, but it did not quite catch on in the same way that the Jack daw, or the Robin redbreast or the Mag pie were permanently linked with their affectionate nicknames.

Its slightly puzzling Linnaean name, *Troglodytes*, refers to the fact that the wren usually builds its nest in holes. (See **troglodyte**)

xylophone

How do you tell the difference between a xylophone and a glockenspiel?

It's a matter of materials. If the bars are made of wood, it is a xylophone, getting its name from Greek *xylon*, 'wood' and *phone*, 'sound'. A glockenspiel, on the other hand, is made up of metal bars or bells, and uses the German words *Glocke*, 'bell' and *Spiel*, 'play'. *(See **cloche**)*

ye

The 'ye' that you sometimes see in pseudo-archaic shop-signs such as 'Ye Olde Tea Shoppe', looks phoney, and is, on the face of it, incomprehensible. Why 'ye'?

In Anglo-Saxon there used to be a single letter to represent the 'th' sound. It was called a 'thorn' and written þ. As time went on, it appeared in manuscripts looking more and more like the letter 'y'. Even after the thorn had dropped out of use, this 'y' was kept in abbreviating words beginning 'th', so that 'them' was written 'y^m', 'that' was written 'y^t' and 'the', of course, was written 'y^e'. So 'ye' is just the definite article 'the'.

yob

It might not be obvious to everybody that 'yob' is simply 'boy' spelt backwards.

It is part of the old Cockney 'backslang' used by London thieves and beggars, in which words were reversed and sometime extra syllables added, so that other people within hearing could not understand what these rogues were saying.

A 'top o' reeb' would be a 'pot of beer'. And 'Cool ta the dillo namo' would be 'Look at the old woman'!

zany

This semi-slang word has an honourable history in the world of the theatre, that takes us back to the Commedia dell'Arte, a popular improvised style of comedy that flourished in Italy from the sixteenth until the eighteenth century.

One of the several alternative names for it was *commedia dei zanni*. The *zanni* (meaning literally 'johnnies' – the word is a form of *Giovanni*, John) were the quick-witted servants who played an important part in these comedies. Harlequin himself, the lover of Columbine, is derived from one of these *zanni*.

The word developed into English 'zany'. In the Elizabethan theatre, a zany was a buffoon of a servant attending an acrobat or clown; he would try incompetently to ape his master's acrobatics. We see a reference to him in Ben Jonson's *Every man out of his Humour* (IV, 1) where Macilente says:
"for indeed
He's like the zany to a tumbler
That tries tricks after him to make men laugh."

From its meaning of 'clumsy imitator', the word acquired the sense 'clownish, idiotic', until we now have the modern 'zany comedy' – linguistically if no longer culturally very close to the original *commedia dei zanni*.

zest

To do something with zest means to act with energy and enthusiasm. But where did the word come from?

The original meaning of 'zest' is orange-peel, or lemon-peel. Pieces of it were used in preserving, to add flavour, and oil pressed from the peel was added to wine to give it extra 'relish'.

zodiac

The connection of this word with 'zoo' may not immediately be apparent. The 'zoo' part of the more formal name, 'zoological gardens' comes from Greek *zoon*, an animal. *Zoon* had a diminutive form *zodion*, which was used for the animals or signs of the *zodiakos kuklos* (the 'zodiac circle' or for short, 'zodiac') – the belt of the heavens within which the motions of sun, moon and planets seemed to take place.

This belt or 'zodiac' was divided into twelve signs – Aries the ram, Taurus the bull, and so on – and the sun passed through one of these 'signs of the zodiac' each month.

OVERSEAS CHEESE

Many foreign place-names are to be found on the cheese-board. But do you know exactly where the towns and villages are? Here are just a few:

Brie	from the region of Brie, east of Paris, France
Camembert	Originally from the village of Camembert in the Orne Département, France, but now equally well made in the Calvados Département and other parts of Normandy
Emmenthal	from the district of that name in Switzerland
Gorgonzola	from a town a few miles east of Milan, Italy
Gruyère	from the Gruyère district near Lake Geneva, Switzerland
Gouda	from Holland, north east of Rotterdam
Parmesan	from the town of Parma in Northern Italy
Pont L'Evêque	from the district of that name in Normandy, France
Port-Salut	originally made by the monks of the Trappist Monastery of Port-du-Salut in the Mayenne Département, France
Roquefort	from a village of that name in the Cevennes mountains in the Aveyron Département, France

PLACE-NAMES ON THE CHEESE-BOARD

Almost every cheese gets its name from the village, town or district where it was originally made. Caerphilly is in Glamorgan, Wales; Cheddar is in Somerset; Wensleydale comes from North Yorkshire.

It may surprise you to find that stilton cheese was never made in the little village of Stilton in Cambridgeshire, after which it is named. Stilton Cheese was made by Leicestershire farmers, who used to take their produce to the Bell Inn, Stilton, from where it would be taken down to London.

Stilton lies conveniently on the A1 – the 'Great North Road'.

WORDS FROM PEOPLE

AN EXTRAORDINARY NUMBER OF EXTRA EPONYMS

What a lot of words come from surnames! A person whose name passes into the language is called an 'eponym' and the word itself is said to be 'eponymous' – deriving from the Greek *epi*, upon; and *onyma*, a name.

Here's a list of people who enjoy a kind of anonymous fame. We use their names, hardly remembering the shadowy figures who have this strange immortality.

*(Words marked * are also dealt with in the text of this book)*

Anders Ångstöm	(1814-1874) A Swedish physicist from whose name we derive the *angstrom*, a unit of spectroscopical length.
St Audrey	(d. 679) An abbess of Ely: giving us *tawdrey**
André Ampère	(1775-1836) French physicist who gives us the word *amp*.*
Claude Aubriet	(1665-1742) French artist and painter: *aubretia*.
Sir Donald Bailey	(b. 1901) designer of the World War II *Bailey bridges*.
Leslie Hore-Belisha	(d. 1957) British Minister of Transport 1934-37, who first devised pedestrian crossings with *Belisha beacons*.
Lázló Biro	Hungarian inventor of the ball-point pen, the *biro*.*
Amelia Bloomer	(1818-1894) American campaigner for women's rights, who urged women to wear knickerbockers for cycling: *bloomers*.*
Simon Bolivar	(1783-1830) Venezuelan nobleman, 'the Liberator' of six South American countries. *Bolivia* is named after him.
Thomas and William Bowler	Nineteenth-century London hat-makers who designed the *bowler hat* in 1850.
Dr Thomas Bowdler	(1754-1825) an English physician who published an expurgated version of Shakespeare in 1818: *bowdlerise*.
Captain Charles Boycott	(d. 1897) An Irish land agent whose uncompromising attitudes led to his being *boycotted* by his neighbours.
Louis Braille	(1809-52) Blinded as a child, he invented the famous Braille alphabet of embossed dots.
Robert Bunsen	(1811-99) A German chemist who lost an eye in a laboratory explosion, and subsequently invented the *Bunsen burner*.
Lord Cardigan	(1797-1868) English aristocrat: popularised the *cardigan*.*

Anders Celsius — (1701-1744) Swedish astronomer and professor at Uppsala University who devised the *Celsius* scale of temperature in 1742.

Nicholas Chauvin — Born in Rochefort, France. A fanatical supporter of Napoleon. His name has been adopted to signify *chauvinism*.*

William Clark — (d. 1838) US army captain and explorer: the flower *clarkia*.

Dr. Anders Dahl — (d. 1789) Swedish botanist, pupil of Linnaeus: *dahlia*. The flower is said to have been named because it resembled Dahl's long untidy hair.

Lord Derby — (b. 1752) English aristocrat who founded two famous horse races: the Oaks and the Derby.

Thomas Derrick — (working in London about 1600) A notorious public executioner hanging people at Tyburn, where Marble Arch is today. His name gives us the *derrick*, a crane or hoist, especially on ships.*

Rodolf Diesel — (1858-1913) German engineer who invented the *diesel* engine.

Duns Scotus — (c.1266-1308) Scottish thinker, whose name has, rather unjustly, added the word *dunce* to our language.*

Vlad Dracula — (d. 1462) A blood-thirsty ruler of what is nowadays Romania. Known as 'The Impaler' for obvious, horrible reasons.

Dracon — (7th cent. BC) An Athenian who devised a legal code in which death was the usual punishment. His name gives us *draconian*.

Daniel Fahrenheit — (1686-1736) Danish instrument-maker, who invented the thermometer which was based on mercury rather than alcohol.

Guy Fawkes — (executed 1606) Tried to blow up Parliament in 1605. Was discovered, tried, executed, and subsequently burnt in effigy every 5 November. ('Penny for the Guy'). And his name gives rise to the casual term '*guy*' for 'man'.

William Forsyth — (1737-1804) English botanist and gardener to King George III. The yellow flower *forsythia* is named after him.

Leonard Fuchs — (1501-66) German botanist, whose name is remembered in the many varieties of *fuchsia* plants.

Giuseppe Garibaldi — (1807-1882) Italian patriot who unified Italy. He liked 'squashed fly' biscuits and had them made for him. They have been given his name ever since.

Richard Gatling	(d. 1903) US inventor of the *Gatling-gun.*
Hans Geiger	(d. 1945) German physicist who invented the *geiger counter* to measure radio-active disintegration.
Dr. Joseph Guillotin	(1738-1814) French professor of anatomy who proposed that death-sentences on all classes of people should be carried out using the machine which now bears his name.*
Heinrich Hertz	(1857-94) German physicist whose name appears on every list of radio wavelengths. He invented a way to measure frequencies.
Thomas Hobson	(c.1544-1631) A famous Cambridge carrier who hired out his horses strictly in rotation, always the one nearest to the stable-door. *Hobson's choice* came to mean no choice at all!
Patrick Hoolihan	(late 19th Cent.) Irish London-dweller, whose riotous family has immortalised him in the word *hooligan.**
Jules Léotard	(1830-70) French trapeze artist whose name is on the lips of all gymnasts who wear *leotards* for their various activities.*
Isaac Newton Lewis	(b. 1858) US army colonel, inventor of the *Lewis gun.*
Charles Lynch	(d. 1796) Virginian captain and magistrate, whose rough and illegal executions gives us the verb '*to lynch*'.
John McAdam	(1756-1836) Scottish engineer, whose *macadamised* surfaces revolutionised our roads and road-making.
Ernest Mach	(d. 1916) Austrian physicist whose name is perpetuated in the speed of sound: for example, Concorde reaches *Mach* 2.
Niccolo Machiavelli	(1469-1527) An Italian diplomat who wrote the famous book *Il Principe*, in which unscrupulous political cunning is presented as the proper way to succeed: *Machiavellian* scheming.
Charles Macintosh	(1766-1843) A Scottish chemist who invented a rubberised solution to make cloth waterproof. We still wear *mackintoshes.**
Mae West	(b. 1893) American film star with huge personal attractions. World War II pilots named their inflatable life jackets after her: *mae wests.*
Pierre Magnol	(1638-1715) French botanist after whom the *magnolia* is named.*
Colonel Martinet	(d. 1676) Ferociously-severe French army officer, whose strict discipline is still remembered in the word *martinet.*

Leopold von Sacher-Masoch (1836-1895) An Austrian novelist who described the curious pleasure gained by self-torture: *masochism*.

Mausolus (d. 353 BC) King of Caria whose magnificent tomb was one of seven wonders of the world. *Mausoleums* are named after this.*

Samuel Maverick (d. 1870) A Texan cattle-farmer, whose unbranded animals strayed onto neighbours' land. These *mavericks* were quickly seized and branded by other farmers, claiming them for themselves.

Dame Nellie Melba (1861-1931) Australian operatic soprano whose singing was greatly admired. The dessert *Peach Melba* is named after her.*

Franz Mesmer (1734-1815) Austrian physician whose theory of 'animal magnetism' led to *mesmerism*, an early form of hypnotism.

Sir William Mills (1856-1932) Inventor of the World War I *Mills bomb*.

Samuel Morse (1791-1872) American Professor of Art and Design who invented the *morse code*. The first message, 'What God hath wrought', was sent in 1844 between Baltimore and Washington.

Jean Nicot (born 1530) French ambassador at Lisbon, who enjoyed the newly-discovered tobacco. He sent some back to France, praising it as the 'medical herb'. *Nicotine* is named after him.

Peter Nissen (1871-1930) A Canadian army colonel who designed the first *Nissen hut* to shelter troops in World War I.

Louis Pasteur (1822-95) French chemist whose process of sterilising milk is remembered in *pasteurised* milk.

Anna Pavlova (1885-1931) Russian ballerina after whom the *Pavlova* dessert, (meringue filled with fruit and cream) is named.

Samuel Plimsoll (1824-98) An English MP for Derby, who campaigned for legislation to make ships safer and more sea-worthy. The *Plimsoll Line* is named after him – and also *plimsolls*, as the original design on the sole resembled the Plimsoll Line on ships.

Joel Poinsett (1779-1851) American Minister to Mexico who raised the *poinsettia* plant from that country, and introduced it to the rest of the world.

Vidkun Quisling (b. 1887) Norwegian traitor who collaborated with the German occupiers of Norway in World War II. He was executed after the war, and his name has simply come to mean 'traitor'.

Lord Raglan (1788-1855) English commander in the Crimean War. He had lost his right arm at the Battle of Waterloo, and so devised the *raglan sleeve* to help him to get his overcoat off and on.*

César Ritz (b. 1850) A poor Swiss peasant who rose from rags to riches and founded the *Ritz Hotels*, renowned for being so *ritzy*.

President Theodore Roosevelt (1858-1919) American President who spared the life of a bear cub when hunting in Mississippi in 1902. His nickname was 'Teddy', and the incident, used in a famous political cartoon, led to the introduction of '*teddy bears*'.*

Marquis de Sade (1740-1814) French aristocrat and madman. Wrote novels in which cruelty gave perverted sexual pleasure: *sadism*.*

Lord Sandwich (1718-92) The fourth Earl of Sandwich was such a keen gambler that he could not bear to waste time eating proper meals. His invention of sliced cold meat between pieces of bread gives us the universally-useful *sandwich*.*

Adolphe Sax (1814-94) Belgian instrument-maker who invented not only the *saxophone*, but also the lesser-known *saxhorn* and *saxtuba*.

General Henry Shrapnel (1761-1842) English army officer who invented the 'spherical case shot' – later (1852) to be called *shrapnel shells*.*

Etienne de Silhouette (1709-1769) French Finance Minister, unpopular for making spending cuts. A *silhouette* is the cheapest way of making a drawing or painting. Hence the name of these black cut-outs.*

Giovanni Spinetti (lived about 1500) made the earliest *spinets* – early forms of harpsichord.

'Little Tich' (early 20th Cent.) A great music-hall comedian and impersonator. His real name was Harry Relph. His stage-name was 'Little Tich', and *tich* has come to mean any diminutive man.

The Rev. William Spooner (1844-1930) English cleric, Warden of New College Oxford, who transposed initial letters, thus creating *spoonerisms*. (see page 56 for some examples)

Vicomte de Turenne (d. 1671) Marshal of France who turned his helmet into a soup-bowl, thus (perhaps) creating a *tureen*.

Admiral Edward Vernon (1684-1757) English naval commander who always wore a coat of coarse cloth called 'grogram'. * (See **grog**, **groggy**).

Queen Victoria (1819-1901) Many places have been named after her. She is also commemorated in the *victoria plum* and the *victoria sponge-cake*.

Count Alessandro Volta (1745-1827) Italian physicist and inventor of the electric battery. He is remembered in the word *volt*.

James Watt (1736-1819) Scottish inventor, mostly associated with steam-engines (he first used the term 'horse-power').

	Long after his death, in the 1880s his name became used as the unit of electrical power, the *watt*.
Duke of Wellington	(1769-1852) English victor at Waterloo. His name is now for ever linked with *wellies (wellington boots)* and with the gigantic Californian tree, the Sequoia *Wellingtonia*.
William Yapp	(Mid 19th Cent.) London bookseller. Invented '*yapped*' books (with leather covers going beyond the edges of the pages) to prevent pages becoming tatty. He used to carry a Bible in his pocket, and *yapping* was the perfect solution to the problem.
Count Ferdinand von Zeppelin	(1838-1917) Inventor of the first airship, named *zeppelins* after him. These *zeppelins* made the first aerial bombing raids, flying over Britain in World War I.

CLOTHING-WORDS AND PLACE-NAMES

Clothes and the material they are made from have often been given their names because of the towns or countries where they were originally made. Can you place all of these on the map?

(words dealt with in the text are marked *)

astrakhan	comes from Astrakhan, near the Caspian sea
balaclava helmets	are names from Balaclava, in the Crimea, Russia, scene of the famous 'Charge of the Light Brigade'.
calico	derives from Calicut on the Malibar coast of India
cravats*	were first worn by 17th century Croat soldiers in Croatia
Crétonne	may be derived from the village of Créton in Normandy
denim	comes from Nîmes in France (de Nîmes)
damask	comes from Damascus in Syria
duffel coats*	came originally from the Belgian town of Duffel
gauze	probably derives its name from the city of Gaza, Palestine
Harris tweed	comes from the Island of Harris, Scotland
jeans*	come from Genoa in Italy
jerseys	unsurprisingly derive from the Channel Island of Jersey
milliners	derive their name from Milan, Italy. They were 'Milaners'
muslin	was first made in the city of Mosul, northern Iraq
suède	is simply French for 'Swedish'. It comes from Sweden
worsted	came originally from the Norfolk village of Worstead

WHERE DO ENGLISH WORDS COME FROM?
A BRIEF HISTORY OF THE ENGLISH LANGUAGE

The Celts

When the Romans landed here in 55 BC the native Britons spoke a language which today still survives in the various Celtic tongues.

There were two groups: the Gaelic or Goidelic Celts, whose language is represented in the modern Irish, Scottish Gaelic and Manx (spoken on the Isle of Man); and the Cymric or Britannic Celts, whose language is represented by Welsh, Cornish and French Breton.

These Celtic languages are quite separate from English, and the only words which remain in use in England are found in ancient place-names: *avon*, meaning a river, *aber*, meaning a river mouth, are two of these remote survivals.

The Romans

The Romans began their occupation of Britain in AD 43 and made their final departure about AD 410. Between those dates, they built many towns, based on their original camp-sites.

Latin for 'camp' is castra, and even to this day there are many towns with names ending in 'caster' or 'chester', reminding us of the time of Roman occupation: examples - Manchester, Dorchester, Lancaster, Chichester. But there are virtually no other Roman words coming down to us from that time.

Angles, Saxons, Frisians and Jutes

When the last Roman ship left these shores about 410 AD this was the signal for land-hungry tribesmen of northern Europe to seek their fortunes in the British Isles. Boatload after boatload of eager immigrants came: Angles, Saxons, Jutes, Frisians, Franks. The Anglo-Saxon invasion had begun. The native Britons, or Celts, were pushed further and further into the fringes – into Cornwall, Wales, Scotland. Meanwhile there was a kind of frantic free-for-all as the Saxon invaders seized whatever bits of land they could.
The language they brought with them is known as Anglo-Saxon, or Old English, abbreviated as O.E. in most dictionaries.
The oldest words in our language come from this period. Typically, they are short, pithy, earthy. The names of animals, birds, trees, and the elemental things of life are Anglo-Saxon in origin. Pig, cow, sheep, sun, moon, star, mother, father, water, earth, life, death: all these are Old English words.
There are countless place-names too, dating from this Anglo-Saxon invasion. Typically, a boatload of Saxons would show allegiance to their leader, whose name is still to be found incorporated in the place-name where they eventually settled.

The Saxon word *ingas* meant 'family' or 'followers', so that when a boatload landed, the chief's name (say, Tota, Wocca, Haefer, or Padda) would be perpetuated in the name of the spot where he carved out his little kingdom, and this would be followed by '*-ing*' to show that Tota's family or Wocca's followers had settled there with him. Tooting, Woking, Havering and Paddington are typical examples.

A *ham* meant 'home' or 'homestead' and a *tun* was 'enclosure' and later came to mean 'village' or 'town'. So a village with a name such as Donington would suggest that it was the 'town where Dunna's people live'.

The Christianizing of Britain

Coming from Rome in AD 597 Augustine and forty monks landed in Kent with the firm intention of converting the British to Christianity.

Luckily for Augustine, King Ethelbert of Kent gave him a friendly reception; after all, Ethelbert's wife, Queen Bertha, was already a Christian. Ethelbert himself was soon baptised, and by the time Augustine died, seven years later, the whole of the Kingdom of Kent had become Christian.

The importance of this on our language was that many Latin words, at first mostly connected with the church, but then more general vocabulary, came into use.

Church words from this time include: abbot, alms, altar, candle, disciple, hymn, relic, rule, shrine, temple. More general Latin-derived words then added to our language include: cap, sock, purple, school, lily, plant, anchor, fever.

Scandinavian Invasions: Vikings and Danes

Waves of Scandinavian attacks upon England began in 787.

Although their language was similar to that of the Saxons, there were differences for example in pronunciation. Old English often had a soft 'sh' sound, whilst the Scandinavians had a harder 'sk' sound. Thus, Old English has ship, shall, fish: but words we have taken from the Scandinavians retain the hardness of sky, skin, skill, scrape and scrub.

(Interestingly, Old English has given us 'shirt', whilst the corresponding Old Norse word has come down to us as 'skirt'. Really, versions of the same word.)

Perhaps the clearest evidence of those Viking invasions is to be found in place-names ending in '*-by*', a Danish word meaning a farm or town. We have more than 600 of these - e.g. Derby, Rugby, Grimsby, Whitby. Other Scandinavian place-name elements are *thorpe*, meaning village and *toft*, meaning a farmstead.

Dictionaries usually note these derivations with the abbreviation O.N. (Old Norse).

William the Conqueror brings us Norman French

As everybody knows, 1066 is the momentous date in English history, when Duke William of Normandy beat King Harold at the Battle of Hastings and settled himself on the throne of England as King William I.

The occupation of the British Isles by the Normans had a cataclysmic effect upon the language. What happened was virtually a grafting of one whole language upon another. And, of course, Norman French itself was largely based on Latin.

It took centuries for the two languages to fuse together completely, but the final result was that today our language has an enormous vocabulary – literally twice as large as most others. We have an exceptionally large choice of alternatives, usually one set of words based on our Anglo-Saxon heritage and another based on Latin/Norman French.

Even those elemental words, pig, cow, sheep, have alternatives. It has wryly been observed that these animals retain their Saxon names when in the fields, looked after by the Saxon peasants, but were given Norman names when they were cooked and served up to the Norman overlords: pig into pork, cow into beef, sheep into mutton, calf into veal, deer into venison.

If you refer back to that list given on page 129, giving examples of basic Saxon short words, you can see how Saxon is paralleled by Latin: the Old English 'sun' has the Latin-based adjective 'solar'; 'moon' has 'lunar'; 'star' has 'stella'. Subtle differences emerged. 'Motherly' is not quite the same as 'maternal'; and then what about 'fatherly' – 'paternal', 'watery' – 'aquatic', 'earthy' – 'terrestrial', 'lively' – 'vital, and 'deathly' – 'mortal?

There is a built-in richness about a language containing so many alternatives.

'Old English' changes into 'Middle English'

Language historians call the language used by the Saxons 'Old English' up to about the year 1150 AD. By that time the fusion of Saxon and Norman French was beginning to form a new language: and this, spoken and written from about 1150 to 1500, is known as 'Middle English' – often abbreviated as M.E. in dictionaries.

Probably the most famous English writer in the Middle Ages was Chaucer (1340-1400), who was writing his *Canterbury Tales* in the 1380s. This is written in 'Middle English', and although it looks strange at first sight, modern readers can usually come to read and understand it without too much difficulty. 'Old English', on the other hand, needs a specialist to make sense of it.

By about 1500 English had become almost 'modern', although of course the spellings were often very different, and the vocabulary was naturally smaller than that of present-day English because it dealt with a much simpler life-style.

Additions from everywhere

The story of English from 1500 onwards is one of constant growth. Explorers discovered new lands, containing new plants (potato, tomato, tulip), new animals (hippopotamus, giraffe, kangaroo), new foods and drinks (tea, coffee, rum). Thinkers re-discovered Greek words and ideas (democracy, aristocracy, equator). Religious reformers needed new words for new concepts (transubstantiation, mystical, agnosticism). And finally, the great artists and scientists added word after word as their experiments led them into new dimensions of thought.

It is interesting to note the first usages of words, as they record the very growth of human consciousness. 'Evaporate' was first used in 1545, 'vacuum' 1550, 'parabola' 1579, 'skeleton' 1578, 'mosquito' 1583, 'laboratory' 1605, 'atmosphere' 1638, 'gravity' 1641, 'microscope' 1656, 'stalagmite' 1681.

The large Oxford English Dictionary gives thousands of 'firsts' like these. There are many surprises: for example, the word 'agnostic' was 'invented' one evening in 1869 by the Victorian thinker, T. H. Huxley.

Today and beyond

This process of assimilation continues. The English language seems to have an unquenchable thirst for new words.

New methods of rapid communication, together with the ever-growing complexities of the computer world and the Internet, are producing virtually an extra new language. Our desks are cluttered with faxes, modems and mouses (or should we still speak of 'mice'?).

And English has spread throughout the world, becoming what is for all practical purposes an international language. Equipped with even a smattering of English, you can be understood virtually everywhere.

This voracious, vital and vibrant language has a fascinating past. The future will certainly see many further changes. It will never stay still.